TROUT
— FISHING TACTICS —

Concept Manager
Bill Classon

Editors
Jim Harmon, Helen McMahon, Rick Keam

Contributors
Stephen Booth, Bill Classon, Greg French, Bill James,
Fred Jobson, Bill Presslor, Steve Starling, Wayne
Tempest, Steve Williamson

Contributing Photographers
David Roche, Greg French, Bill Classon, Micah Adams,
Chris Parkinson, Lee Rayner

Illustrations
Trevor Hawkins

Designer
Neetu Patel

Published and distributed by
Australian Fishing Network
48 Centre Way
Croydon South, Vic. 3136
Telephone (03) 9761 4044   Facsimile (03) 9761 4055
Email: sales@afn.com.au
Website: www.afn.com.au

ISBN 18651 3080X

All rights reserved
First published 2005

Contents

Introduction

Freshwater Fishing has now become a very diverse and popular pastime. Over the past twenty years there have been myriads of new lakes and impoundments that have opened offering all sorts of new angling possibilities. Additionally, there has been enormous growth in new fisheries, especially through the stocking of trout in so many of our rivers and impoundments.

New techniques and tactics have been developed to catch these trout all year round and the pages in this book will show you how to master these techniques to catch more trout. This book cuts straight to the chase. Each chapter has been written by an expert in the field and each author contributes to *Freshwater Fishing Australia* magazine. Their style is to present information in an easy to understand manner regardless of how technically complex the subject.

All the writers are practical hands-on anglers with years of experience in their field and on the water. None have held back on information either—they have even put down their secrets and hard-learned personal strategies.

The subjects covered include trolling and all its variations, lure casting and its strategies and options, all the baits available and how to fish them and a complete description of our trout species. No matter where you fish for trout or how you fish for trout there is plenty of information for you here in an easy to understand and informative layout.

All up there's everything you need to know about every aspect of catching trout. All the tips, systems and tactics in a series of informative chapters including downrigging, flatline trolling, lead core trolling, side planing, lurecasting and baitfishing. As our chapter contributors are amongst the best angling authors in Australia, there is a bright, readable and enjoyable style that will make you thirsty to apply the methods.

All in all the information will enhance all trout anglers' knowledge and will help everyone to become a more successful trout angler.

The Trout

Salmonids have been established in the Antipodes for well over a century now. They are the indispensable mainstay of New Zealand and southern Australia's freshwater fisheries. They involve so many widely different people in one of the most socially accepted recreations, build bridges between city and country, help underpin local economies, and motivate anglers to safeguard and improve the environment. No other fish family has ever given more people more pleasure.

Though dominated by brown and rainbow trout, the salmonid family in Australasia also includes brook trout, chinook (quinnat) salmon and Atlantic salmon, and hybrids such as our tiger trout. The various photos on p. 7 show not only some differences between species, but also differences between individuals of the same species dependent on location and environment.

Brown trout are Australia's most prolific trout and generally account for 90% of all recreational captures.

Trout Tales (Tails)

Just to show how things can get confusing have a look at these trout tails and pick the odd one out.

| Rainbow Trout Bullen Merri - Vic | Rainbow Trout Eucumbene - NSW | Brown Trout Lake Youd - Tas | Brown Trout L. Geehi - NSW | Brown Trout Tasmania | Atlantic Salmon Jindabyne - NSW | Tiger Trout N.Z. | Chinook Salmon Purrumbete - Vic |

YES! It's the western lakes, Lake Youd brown trout! Brown trout are generally acknowledged not to have spots on their tail. There's always an exception to the rule and have a good look at this Tasmanian western lakes "spotty tailed" from First Lagoon. This area in Tasmania is one of the few in the world where browns have spots on their tails. **WHAT A TALE!**

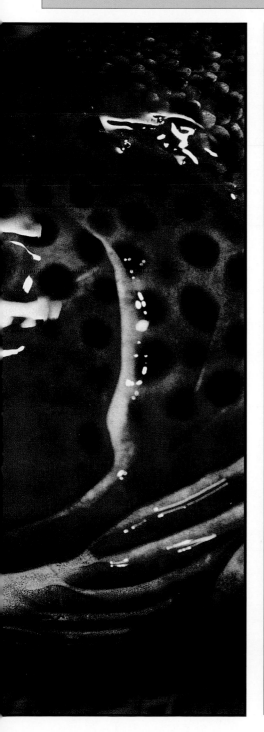

COLOUR OF TROUT

Brown Trout - Geehi Dam NSW.

Rainbow Trout - Merri River - Vic.

Triploid Rainbow Trout - Tasmania

Rainbow Trout - Cox's River - NSW

Rainbow Trout - Lake Murdeduke Vic.

Brook Trout - Lake Rolleston - Tasmania

Brown Trout - Tasmania

Brown Trout - Lake Jindabyne NSW.

Atlantic Salmon (River) - Tasmania

Atlantic Salmon - Tasmania

Brown Trout *(Salmo trutta)*

The brown trout is perhaps the most respected of all freshwater sportfish. It thrives in a great diversity of habitats—oceans, estuaries, rivers, small streams, coastal lagoons and alpine lakes— and has a much varied diet. Since it is more wary than other trout species and can be relatively difficult to fool, it is highly prized by skilled anglers.

Brown Trout - River

Native Range

Brown trout are native to mainland Europe, the British Isles, Iceland, the Caspian Sea, the Black Sea, the Aral Sea, Turkey, Afghanistan and the Atlas Mountains in northern Africa.

Introduction to Australia and New Zealand

In 1864 a shipment of 100,000 Atlantic salmon arrived in Hobart from Britain, along with a last minute gift of several thousand brown trout. This was the first successful transportation of salmonids to the South Pacific, the culmination of years of effort by mainly commercial interests. Ultimately the salmon failed to acclimatise yet the brown trout proved very successful and their progeny were soon transported to mainland Australia and New Zealand.

In hindsight, trout from the initial consignment would have been sufficient to establish the species, yet in subsequent years numerous importations to Tasmania were documented. Among these were other 'strains' of brown trout including sea trout and Loch Leven trout.

Likewise, the fact that robust populations of trout quickly established in New Zealand from the original Tasmanian stock did little to dissuade local authorities from securing additional ova from Tasmania and various European countries.

Current Distribution in Australasia

The species is not well adapted to warm water and is absent from Queensland and the Northern Territory as well as most of South Australia and Western Australia.

However, the success of the species in temperate Australasia has been astounding. Today, thriving populations are found throughout New Zealand, Tasmania and in the cooler regions of Victoria and New South Wales. Self supporting stocks are also found in the south-western corner of

Brown Trout - Western Lakes

Western Australia and the highlands of New Guinea. The limited stocks in South Australia are primarily maintained by artificial stocking.

Spawning

In Australasia spawning is primarily a winter event. All brown trout, including sea run fish and estuary dwellers, spawn in freshwater. Most lake fish migrate upstream, though outflows are used if other facilities are poor. Shore spawning is uncommon. Sea trout migrate into rivers and tributaries, while river residents usually spawn close to their home territory.

Growth and Size

In heavily populated waters, where there is a lot of competition for food and space,

Brown Trout - Lake

young fish (especially those which have never spawned) out-compete older fish. Consequently, trout in these waters gain little weight after first spawning and most fish live for just three to five years. However where there is little competition for food longevity is common. The maximum life span is in the order of 20 years.

Brown trout in the Caspian Sea can attain 1.4 m in length and 50 kg, though I have never read of these fish in angling literature. The biggest brown trout caught on a rod and line was 39 1/2 pounds (18 kg). Fish in excess of 17 kg have been taken in New Zealand and the biggest officially recorded in Tasmania weighed 28 3/4 lb. (about 13 kg).

Sea Run Versus River Resident Brown Trout

Brown Trout, Sea Run - Merri River Victoria

Brown Trout, River - Merri River Victoria

Rainbow Trout
(Oncorhynchus mykiss)

In Australia rainbow trout are less common than browns and retain a certain mystique. They are often very aggressive and statistically they are relatively easy to catch (though any experienced angler will soon let you know that they can often be as difficult to fool as any other salmonid). The species is renowned for its strength, being noted for its long runs with the line and tendency to leap high out of the water.

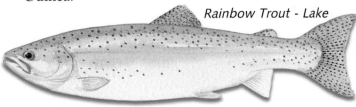

Rainbow Trout - River

Native Range
Rainbows are native to the west coast of North America, the Mackenzie River drainage (which flows north from central Canada to the Arctic Ocean), and the Kamchatka Peninsula in south-eastern Siberia.

Introduction to New Zealand and Australia
Rainbow trout may have been introduced to New Zealand as early as 1877, though the most important shipment arrived there in 1883 from California (being sourced from the McCloud River, the Russian River or Sonoma Creek). From New Zealand the species was transferred to New South Wales (1894), Victoria (1898), Tasmania (1898) and Western Australia (1907).

Current Distribution in Australasia
While the range of rainbow trout in Australasia more or less duplicates that of the brown trout, the relative success of each species differs from water to water. The most prominent fisheries are found in the North Island of New Zealand, though major populations also occur throughout the South Island, Tasmania, the temperate parts of Victoria and New South Wales, the south west corner of Western Australia, and in the highlands of New Guinea.

Rainbow Trout - Lake

Spawning
In Tasmania, most (if not all) fish spawn in spring. On mainland Australia spawning migrations at some rivers (including the Cox's River) commence early in winter. The runs at New Zealand's most famous fisheries (like Taupo and Rotorua) reach a furious peak in winter but sometimes continue in dribs and drabs throughout the year.

Spawning rainbows prefer to utilise gravelly tributary creeks but will use other sites when necessary. Some lake populations are maintained entirely by shore spawning.

Rainbows in Rivers and Streams
River fish like swift flowing environments and cold water, and rarely do well in warmish lowland streams.

In Tasmania thriving populations of riverine rainbows have become extinct following the introduction of brown trout and there are only a few streams where the two species coexist. The success of rainbow trout in these waters may be due to flow regimes being both atypical and better suited to the later-spawning rainbows.

The experience in the south-east of mainland Australia has been very similar to that in Tasmania with rainbows being mainly confined to highland waters.

Western Australia is almost unique in having significant wild populations of rainbow trout in lowland rivers. There has long been speculation that these fish might propagate successfully if transferred to lowland waters in south-eastern Australia. However, they are not an unusual strain of fish and their success is most likely due to the fact that they live in waters where flows at spawning time are especially well suited to the species. Also there is often little competition from brown trout and many fisheries are maintained by intensive stocking regimes.

In New Zealand's big cold headwater streams rainbows commonly out-compete browns, apparently finding the swift-flow habitat much to their liking.

Rainbow Trout in Lakes
Lake populations of rainbows tend to be less fickle than riverine populations and most highland waters are able to support significant numbers of both species. Two factors are at work here. First, competition for space is less intense. Second, the two species prefer different micro-habitats, with rainbows generally avoiding the shallow marshes so well utilised by browns, preferring instead to feed in deep open water and wind lanes.

Brook Trout Char
(Salvelinus fontinalis)

These are perhaps the most easily caught of all salmonids and are generally regarded as inferior fighters. Nonetheless, the species is very rare here and has enduring novelty value.

Native Range
The stronghold is the east coast of North America from the Arctic Circle to New England. Other native populations are found further south in the Appalachian Mountains.

Spawning and Growth
The preferred spawning habitat is shallow water with low flow and the species is especially attracted to springs and upwellings. Some lake populations are maintained entirely by shore spawning on beaches.

Brook Trout - Male

Brook Trout - Female

Brook trout commonly mature early in life—males at one year, females at two—and where competition is high they make little growth in subsequent years. Consequently populations in small streams commonly comprise stunted individuals no bigger than 200 millimetres. In lakes and big rivers, however, very good sizes can be attained. The largest fish I know of weighed 14 1/2 lb. (about 6.6 kg) and was taken in 1916 from the Nipigon River in Ontario (Canada).

Difficulty of Acclimatisation
Within its natural range the brook trout has been unable to withstand competition from non-native trout. Rainbows have been identified as the most serious threat, but this may only be because the species has been so widely translocated—brown trout are known to have eliminated some riverine populations.

It is hardly surprising then that in Australasia brook trout have established and prevailed only in waters which have remained free of browns and rainbows.

Brook Trout in New Zealand
Brook trout were imported to New Zealand from the eastern United States last century, probably in 1877 and 1887, resulting in widespread releases and healthy hatchery brood stock.

Brook trout were stocked into Lake Emily (in the South Island at Mt. Sommers) in 1932 and 1938 resulting in a wild population which persists even now, offering anglers the chance to take fish in excess of 3 kilograms. The upper Hinemania Dam (in the Taupo district in the North Island) was stocked in 1952 and now gives up plenty of wild fish in the 1–2.5 kg range.

Brook Trout in New South Wales
The first 1000 brook trout ova to arrive in New South Wales came from New Zealand in 1890. Subsequently 200 fish were turned out into Barbers Creek Reservoir but they failed to breed.

The modern history of the species in New South Wales began in 1968 when a gift of 5000 ova was received from Tasmania, 4000 of which went to the Gaden Hatchery and 1000 to the Dutton Hatchery. Brood stock currently held at both hatcheries are progeny of this importation.

Several waters received limited stocks including the Aberfoyle River, the Maclaughlin River, the Queanbeyan River, Copeton Dam and the Snowy River, though returns to anglers were poor and the fish eventually disappeared. Natural recruitment occurred at Ogilvies Creek near Tooma (stocked in 1984 and 1988) but this water is not a major recreational resource.

The best known brook trout fishery is Lake Jindabyne. Here, though, the fish are mainly brood stock released from the Gaden hatchery into the inflowing Thredbo River.

Brook Trout in Tasmania
The first brook trout imported to Tasmania came from New Zealand in 1883. Just a hundred or so healthy yearlings resulted and these were held as brood stock in the Salmon Ponds. The first releases occurred in various waters in 1885. The only viable fishery was at Lake Leake (on the east coast) where from 1889 to 1908 a significant wild population was established. However, rainbow trout were released into the lake in 1904 and soon displaced the brook trout. At about the same time interest in liberating hatchery-reared brook trout in other Tasmanian waters evaporated and the species soon disappeared.

Brook trout were not reintroduced into Tasmania until early 1962 when some 50 000 ova arrived from Nova Scotia (Canada). Fish from this consignment were distributed to several lakes (including Little Pine Lagoon) without success. However, the 100 or so fingerlings placed into Clarence Lagoon (in the Central Highlands) in 1963 established a fragile wild population. In 1979 it was decided to bolster the

Clarence stocks by liberating hatchery-reared fish. Today the fishery is maintained largely by artificial stocking, though wild spawners at the lake continue to be used as a source of ova and milt. Fish taken by anglers average 1 kg with odd ones to 3 or 4 kilo.

In 1983 a power development was approved in a remote area of Tasmania's West Coast where the natural streams and lakes remained trout free. Recognising that the new hydro lakes would be illegally stocked with trout if any attempt was made to keep the area as a reserve for native fauna, the Inland Fisheries Commission resolved to trial brook trout. The first releases occurred in 1986 and, while artificial stocking is at present ongoing, there has also been significant natural spawning. This area, incorporating lakes Plimsoll, Selina and Rolleston, is now the most viable brook trout fishery in Australia, giving up plenty of 1-2 kg fish as well as some in excess of 4 kilograms.

Lake Trout (Salvelinus namaycush) & Sockeye Salmon
(Oncorhynchus nerka)

The mackinaw or lake trout was introduced into New Zealand from Michigan (United States) in 1906 and liberated into two lakes on the South Island. The fish in Lake Grassmere apparently died out in the 1970s but the species maintains a tenuous existence in Lake Pearson. Pearson mackinaw are small and lean, usually weighing just a kilo or so, and are only occasionally taken by anglers (who prefer to target Pearson's magnificent browns and rainbows). The brood stock now held at the Wanaka hatchery are descendant from fish collected at Lake Pearson in 1977.

Fragile landlocked populations of sockeye salmon are established in the South Island in the upper Waitaki system, mainly in Lake Ohau and its tributaries. These fish are descendants of stock introduced into New Zealand from Canada in 1902. The normal size of spawning fish is just 180 - 450 mm in length and the species is not usually targeted by anglers.

Chinook (Quinnat) Salmon
(Oncorhynchus tshawytscha)

The chinook salmon (still sometimes known as quinnat salmon in New Zealand) is one of six species of Pacific salmon. These fish are essentially sea migratory, spending most of their lives in the ocean and returning upstream to their birth-place to spawn and die. Under certain conditions it is possible for some Pacific salmon to establish self-supporting landlocked populations, though such fish rarely attain the weights of their saltwater counterparts.

Quinnat Salmon in New Zealand
In New Zealand, the first importation of quinnat salmon occurred in 1875, with follow-up importations being undertaken over the next four years. These shipments resulted in widespread liberations, though it seems that none were successful.

The forebears of existing New Zealand stock arrived from the McCloud River, California (United States), from 1901 to 1907. During this period some 1.5 million young fish were turned out into the Waitaki system.

The first adult fish returning from the sea were noticed in 1905 and the stripping of wild fish began in 1908. By 1916 the fish had spread to adjacent rivers and runs had established in what are today the other three main salmon rivers—the Rangitata, Rakia and Waimakariri. In subsequent years significant populations took hold in rivers as far south as the Clutha in Otago. Today there are also viable sea run populations in some west coast rivers.

In New Zealand, fish returning from the sea average 6-8 kg though plenty weigh 10-15 kilograms. The biggest specimen caught in New Zealand weighed 29 kg, while in the United States weights of at least 57 kg have been recorded.

The success of quinnat salmon appears to be due (in part at least) to the fact that they do not usually migrate far from the continental shelf and therefore are less likely than Atlantic salmon to become disoriented. Nonetheless, New Zealand remains the only place in the world outside of the natural range where sea runs of the species have established.

In addition to the sea runs, self supporting landlocked populations occur in a dozen or so New Zealand lakes, including Coleridge, Kaniere, Wakatipu, Heron, and Wanaka. These fish compete successfully with browns and rainbows but rarely exceed 3 kilograms.

Chinook Salmon in Victoria
Attempts to import chinook salmon from the United States to Australia were made as early as 1874, and the first viable ova arrived in Victoria in 1876 or 1877. These fry were placed in a number of river systems including the Glenelg, Hopkins, Cape Otway, Yarra, Gippsland and Snowy

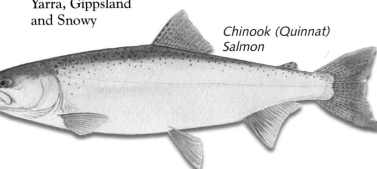

Chinook (Quinnat) Salmon

catchments. It seems that only a few immature salmon were subsequently taken by anglers and that no fish returned from the sea.

Brood fish from the 1877 shipment were held in the Ercildoun hatchery and, while their fate was poorly recorded, the stock ultimately failed both in domestic and wild environments.

The next verifiable shipment occurred in 1936 when 30,000 ova arrived at the Studley Park Hatchery, marking the beginning of regular importations from New Zealand. Although this programme had been initiated to provide alternative sport in Lake Catani (where the trout fishery was failing), fry were immediately liberated at both Lake Catani and Lake Bullen Merri. Lake Purrumbete was stocked in 1937.

Over the next decade at least 18 lakes were seeded with quinnat salmon, though the only worthwhile returns came from lakes Bullen Merri and Purrumbete.

Fry resulting from subsequent shipments (still from New Zealand) were probably all liberated at Bullen Merri and Purrumbete though the programme halted in 1958 due to an unavailability of ova.

Victoria finally secured from the United States gifts of Sacramento River stock in 1963 (all turned out into Purrumbete) and Columbia River stock in 1966. Most of the fry resulting from this last shipment were liberated at Purrumbete but a thousand fish were kept in an earthen dam at Snobs and it is from these fish that Australia's current domesticated brood stock was derived.

In the early 1970s returns from the breeding programmes were just sufficient to maintain the brood stock. It was not until 1976 that enough yearlings (20,000) were available for release into Purrumbete. Stocking of Bullen Merri recommenced in 1978.

Since then chinooks have been trialled at several other waters but with disappointing results until the introduction into the shallow lakes Murdeduke and Modewarre, near Geelong. It is early days yet but their resilience is amazing fisheries managers and they cope with warmer temperatures better than rainbow trout! The key to a successful chinook salmon fishery is a huge forage source and, like Purrumbete and Bullen Merri, these two new venues have just that.

However, it must be recognised that even here, there is no natural recruitment and stocks can only be maintained through regular liberations of hatchery reared fish.

Excluding newly-released fish, most salmon taken in Purrumbete, Murdeduke, Modewarre and Bullen Merri are 1–4 kg but there is always a reasonable chance of taking fish of 6 kg or better.

Quinnat Salmon in Tasmania

The first importation of quinnat salmon to Tasmania occurred in 1902. Some 300,000 fry resulted, of which perhaps 200,000 were released into the Derwent system. A further 850 fish were reared to eight months of age, 200 of which were used to complement the Derwent stocking while the others were scattered in various rivers around the state. None returned from the ocean.

From 1910 to 1917 there were regular importations of ova from New Zealand, resulting in the Derwent receiving annual releases of 12,000–23,000 fry as well as occasional releases of 600–2000 yearlings. Again no adult fish were caught by anglers.

Importations resumed in 1921 and continued until at least 1930 and, while the Derwent received fish during this period, the focus shifted to the River Forth in the north of the State. Again, despite significant annual releases of fry and yearlings, no fish returned from the ocean to either river.

Some 5000 yearlings were turned out into Great Lake in 1931, and over the next couple of years numerous fish to 7 lb (3 kg) were caught but still the species failed to establish.

The last importation was probably that of 25,000 New Zealand ova in 1934. The 10,000 yearlings reared from this batch were taken to Lake St Clair, the Franklin River and the King River but they provided little angling interest and yet again there was no natural recruitment.

Atlantic Salmon
(Salmo salar)

The Atlantic salmon, the 'king of fish', can attain 40 kg or more and is highly sought after by both commercial interests and recreational anglers. In its native range—coastal areas of western Europe and eastern North America—the species is essentially sea migratory, though there are landlocked populations in New England (north-eastern United States) where they are known as sebago salmon. Unlike Pacific salmon, Atlantics do not always die after first spawning and many fish survive to spawn two or even three times.

Atlantic Salmon - Sea run

Difficulty of Acclimatisation in Australasia

Attempts to acclimatise sea running Atlantics in Australasia have failed. The main problem appears to be that our ocean currents are incompatible with the life cycle of the fish. Fish drifting on the currents probably feel the spawning urge when they are far out to sea and then become disoriented and lost. Other poorly understood factors, such as the role of pheromones, also appear to have an effect. I have not read solid scientific evidence of sea runs of Atlantic salmon having established anywhere outside of the fish's normal range though there is anecdotal evidence that sea runs established for a while off the coast of the Chilean lakes district.

Atlantic Salmon - Freshwater

Atlantic Salmon in Tasmania

In Tasmania Atlantic salmon were first introduced in 1864, this being the first successful shipment of live salmonid ova ever to reach the South Pacific. Throughout the rest of the century there were further importations associated with significant attempts to establish the fish (mainly) in the Derwent system. All failed.

In the early 1900s authorities tried to create landlocked populations from sea run fish (Great lake, Lake Leake, the Chudleigh Lakes), again without success. From 1910 to at least 1918 the focus shifted to sebago salmon, though releases in Great Lake, Lake Leake, Lake Dove, and (upper) Arthurs Lake were also doomed to fail.

The Atlantic salmon in Tasmania today are the progeny of domestic sea-strain stock imported from the Gaden hatchery (New South Wales) for commercial sea-cage farming. Most sea cages are anchored off the south-east coast of Tasmania and escapees are regularly taken by recreational anglers fishing either near the cages or in the estuarine reaches of the Huon, Lune, Esperance and D'Entrecasteaux rivers. While these fish have novelty value and are targeted by many, they are not as good a sportfish as the wild sea run brown trout which abound in the same areas. In fact, sea trout and Atlantic salmon can be extremely difficult to differentiate, and many sea trout are erroneously claimed to be salmon.

Major releases of surplus commercial fingerlings were carried out at Great Lake from 1988 to 1990. Few fish grew to more than 1 kg and most were quite lean. There was no natural recruitment.

Atlantic Salmon in New South Wales

In 1963 some 100,000 ova stripped from autumn sea-run fish were imported from Nova Scotia (Canada) and taken to a temporary hatchery near Lake Jindabyne. Of these, some 65,000 hatched and were transferred to the Gaden Hatchery. Other shipments of salmon ova arrived from Nova Scotia in 1964 and 1965 but brood stock were retained only from the 1963 shipment. All Atlantic salmon in Australia today are progeny of this Gaden stock.

The original intention of those responsible for the importations in the 1960s was to find a supply of sebago salmon with which to stock Burrinjuck Dam and its tributaries. In the absence of a source of landlocked fish, sea run salmon were accepted. Fish from all three importations were placed into the Burrinjuck system. While this fishery continues to receive attention (the last release of salmon occurred in 1991) anglers note that the salmon are small and lean and relatively scarce.

Since the mid 1970s most progeny of the Gaden brood fish have been liberated into Lake Jindabyne and the inflowing Thredbo River. At times salmon are seen running up the Thredbo River but no successful spawning has taken place. Anglers stand a reasonable chance of catching Atlantics in the lake but again the fish are rarely in very good condition and the species would soon disappear if artificial stocking ceased.

Experimental liberations of Atlantics into waters such as Copeton Dam and Talbingo have failed to excite anglers or offer reasonable returns.

Atlantic Salmon in New Zealand

In the early 1900s the Waiau River (part of Southland's Lake Te Anau/ Manapouri system) was singled out for intense stocking of Atlantics, the hope being that sea runs might establish if liberations were regular and intense. Success was reported as early as 1916 and by the 1920s the annual catch of Atlantic salmon from the Waiau was in the order of 1000 - 1200 fish. It is now generally accepted that these fish, though originating from sea-run stock, had never run to sea but were either river residents or lake fish migrating downstream from Te Anau.

Rainbow trout were liberated into the lakes in the mid 1920s and by 1929 it was evident that wild

Atlantic salmon in the Waiau were in serious decline. In 1931 anglers were catching one rainbow for every three or four salmon and by 1948 the ratio had reversed.

By the 1970s the Te Anau salmon were all but extinct. Fish were found in lakes Fergus and Gunn in the mid 1970s and in 1976 a redd discovered in the outlet of Lake Fergus yielded enough ova to result in a hundred or so healthy fry. The resulting brood stock is genetically limited but it is all New Zealand has had available in its attempts to secure the species.

Fingerlings have been released into Fergus and Gunn and other waters in the Te Anau system but with limited success, and it is possible that the genetic integrity of any remaining wild stock has been severely compromised.

Hybrids

Most trout and salmon can be successfully crossed and most hybrids are infertile. This method of producing sterile trout does not involve the use of sex-reversed stock (and all the associated drama) and fish so produced often have distinctive patterning and high novelty value.

One of the most notable hybrids is the tiger trout, a fish produced by fertilising brown trout eggs with brook trout milt. This cross invariably results in a high mortality of ova and fry, though the losses can be minimised if the eggs are triploided. Experimental

Tiger Trout

work in Tasmania and New Zealand has shown that tigers grow well and have many of the highly desirable feeding habits of brown trout. They are happy in shallow water and are diverse feeders.

The best tiger trout fishery must surely be Lake Rotoma in the Rotorua district of New Zealand's North Island. Here, the first successful release was made in December 1983 and regular liberations (usually 100 to 1500 fingerlings annually) have been ongoing. Tigers now comprise more than 5% of the annual trout harvest (the rest are rainbows) and three year olds average about 3 kg or so.

In Tasmania tigers have been liberated into the Pet Reservoir. This water is deep and turbid and fish are lost both over the spillway and into the feeder stream. Returns to anglers have been mediocre. Undoubtedly, tigers would provide better sport if released into shallow clearwaters such as some of the (already intensively managed) fisheries in the Nineteen Lagoons.

Another hybrid trialled in Tasmania is a cross between brown trout and Atlantic salmon. These fish are easy to produce (the survival rate of eggs

Triploids

Normal fish are diploids, which is to say that their chromosomes are found in pairs. It is possible to treat freshly fertilised normal eggs in such a way that each pair of chromosomes becomes a triplet. As the cell divides and multiplies, the chromosomes continue to be replicated in triplicate. Resulting fish are sterile but visually indistinguishable from diploids.

Triploid salmonids are produced by applying short heat or pressure shocks to newly fertilised ova. Such treatment often does not result in 100% of the treated eggs being triploided. The greater the shock, the greater the percentage of triploids but greater too the mortality of ova.

Male triploids produce milt (though it is largely infertile) and are subject to normal stresses at spawning time. There is even some evidence to suggest that they can cause minor interference when among normal trout spawners. Females are totally sterile, are not prone to disease at spawning time and display particularly fast growth.

It is possible to produce all-female triploids by shocking eggs that have been fertilised with milt from sex-reversed females. Unfortunately, the creation of sex-reversed brood stock is a messy and costly business. It involves feeding female fry hormone-treated food and then on-growing the stock in the hatchery for several years. As females have no

sperm ducts, each fish must be killed when the time comes to extract the milt.

Fisheries management in Tasmania has favoured rainbow trout for triploids. Part of the reason for this is that triploid research has had a commercial component and historically rainbows have been of most interest to fish farmers. More importantly, though, rainbows are easy to on-grow to fingerling stage. Fish of this size do not become overtly domesticated but are big enough to survive well in the wild.

Triploid rainbows did well in trophy waters in the Nineteen Lagoons. They also performed well when placed among the robust populations of wild trout

in Dee Lagoon. In fact, a few Dee triploids were caught in 1997 — they were eleven years old and weighed 3–5 kg!

It seems that triploid rainbows are no easier to catch than normal rainbows but they are still far more catchable than brown trout. The reality is that most triploid rainbows are killed within one or two years of release — before the advantages of sterility are realised. The benefit of triploid rainbows can only be maximised if anglers are prepared to adopt the catch-and-release philosophy at relevant waters. In waters where anglers are not prepared to release fish, it may be more beneficial to stock with triploid browns and/or sterile hybrids.

Rainbow trout have acclimatised well in Australia. They generally prefer cold, clear, well oxygenated water. They are largely supplemented by hatchery breeding programs as their natural recruitment here in Australia can be haphazard.

and fry is very high) but they are virtually indistinguishable from normal brown trout. They have been released into several reservoirs and minor impoundments but there has been no serious benefit-analysis.

One last hybrid to mention is the splake, a sexually viable cross between mackinaw and brook trout. Splake were produced at the Wanaka hatchery in New Zealand's South Island in 1980 and 1981, with second generation spawnings of male and female splake being carried out in 1983. The hybrid was first released into Lake Dispute near Queenstown but did not reproduce. Further liberations were undertaken at Lake Letitia (North Canterbury) in 1989 and 1992 and, although there is some evidence that splake have spawned here, few fish have been taken by anglers. The future of splake in New Zealand does not look promising. *Greg French & Bill Classon*

Sterile Fish

When salmonids reach maturity they undergo metabolic changes which cause them to lose strength and sturdiness of form. Anyone who has caught maiden (immature) trout of 2 kg or more will testify just how powerful they are — they completely outshine mature fish of the same size.

In the wild most browns and rainbows mature in the third year of life and, where competition for food and space is high, they subsequently find it difficult to compete with younger, stronger fish. Therefore most trout gain little weight after first spawning. Wild fish which somehow delay spawning until the fourth or fifth year are able to dominate weaker fish of the same age and so usually feed well and enjoy continued growth.

What, then, if we liberate hatchery-reared sterile trout into our major sport fisheries?

In some waters, where trout populations are low and there is limited scope for natural recruitment, stocking with hatchery-raised fish has long been an essential management tool. Since competition for food is not intense, even normal trout placed into such fisheries are likely to grow large. The advantages of putting sterile fish into these trophy waters are that such fish have the potential to live longer and grow stronger than their fertile counterparts. Since they feed throughout the year, sterile fish can also attain optimum size relatively quickly.

Stocking with sterile fish is not a suitable management option for all fisheries. Sterile fish have been trialled successfully in suitable waters in both Australia and New Zealand.

Freshwater Baits

When the going gets tough switching to a properly presented live bait usually makes all the difference. Even anglers skilled at other methods know that nothing can match the smell, allure and texture of the real thing .

The key to successful angling is acquiring the bait. Unfortunately, most many new anglers fall into the trap of going on a fishing trip ill-equipped, without any thought of providing decent bait—either alive or dead.

The main problem seems to be that catching live bait can require as much thought and be as time consuming as catching the fish. But catching live bait is almost as enjoyable as going fishing with it! You soon develop an ability to pick waters that hold mudeyes, shrimp, yabbies, minnows etc, and you'll generally find that local creeks, streams and dams are a good source of live baits. Waters in the suburbs can hold better stocks than those in the country where agricultural poisons are commonly used.

A variety of tackle is required to catch baits. A mudeye net and a good quality live bait trap are just the start; a shrimp net, a yabby trap and live bait containers with aerators can also be added, though even this list could be extended.

Nothing can match energetic live bait. A trout with a full belly may ignore a school of galaxiids yet still pounce on a minnow struggling on a hook.

Regularly inspect your bait too, and if it stops swimming or wriggling, replace it. Don't stick with worms that 'just' wriggle or minnows that 'just' swim- get plenty of action into your bait. The vibrations caused by this activity attract the predators.

Always use matched tackle. Don't use a heavy line that will kill the action of your bait. You should rarely need anything but 2 or 3 kg line when bait fishing for trout. It won't impair the delicate swimming action of a mudeye, and is generally strong enough to cope with most trout.

Tackle should be tailored to the bait fishing requirements. The 'mudeye' rod is an example. As the

The best way to set up your outfits for bait fishing is to place them in rod holders that make them close to horizontal as possible. This way the bail arm can be opened to allow the trout to run and take the bait before hookup.

baits are fairly delicate and often require a long drop between float and hook, for lakes a 2.4-2.6 m medium action rod is required. For rivers a shorter version at 2.1 m is perfect.

There is a real finesse to fishing freshwater baits, often more so than their saltwater equivalents. The bait angler has at his disposal a multitude of floats, lines, hooks, sinkers and clips but if the line is too heavy, the hook too big or the float incorrectly weighted, then a fish will ignore the most appetising of baits.

Many anglers prefer naturally clear or brown line for their bait fishing—it has proven its all-round adaptability again and again.

The range of floats available is huge—quills, bobbers, bubbles, corks, styrene and slip bobbers—and all have their uses. Add to this the huge array of coarse angling floats such as wagglers, onions, sticks and stem floats and a float for every fishing situation can be found.

As far as sinkers go, always avoid using lead at all—it is far better to get your bait to swim down naturally to the fish. However, ranges of ball sinkers and split shot are required when circumstances dictate some judicious use of lead.

Hooks are the cheapest item in the tackle box and absolutely the most important. Fine, chemically sharpened hooks are essential when bait fishing.

Mudeyes

The mudeye is an aquatic insect, the nymphal stage of the dragonfly. It varies in colour from dark brown to pale green and in size from 1–4 cm long.

It inhabits the still water of ponds, dams and lakes, mainly in the weeds but also under rocks, submerged trees and other cover. Most importantly the water in which it lives must not be polluted in any way. The slightest hint of agricultural sprays will drastically affect the populations of the mudeyes.

There are basically two types of mudeye—the couta and the spider (or bug) mudeye. The bigger couta mudeye is often the more sought after as it is a more active swimmer however, at times trout show a distinct preference for the spider.

The time to collect mudeyes from ponds and dams is from late winter through to spring and early summer. Once the hot weather

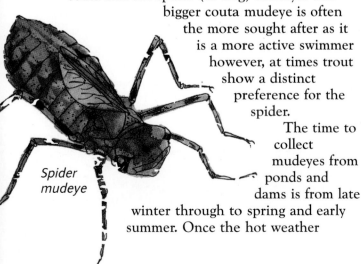

Spider mudeye

comes, the mudeyes will hatch into dragonflies, so get your stocks prior to Christmas and keep them cool for the rest of the season.

Small dams and ponds are ideal places to look for mudeyes. The best method of extracting mudeyes from a pond is to push a 'mudeye net' through the weed, scooping or dragging it near the bottom to collect plenty of weed and debris with each scoop. Then up-end it on the bank close to the water so that you can search through the extracted weed for the mudeyes. A good dam can produce up to a dozen mudeyes per scoop; a dam that has been affected by sprays will be lucky to have any and another dam must be tried.

Couta mudeye

Mudeye nets come in two styles—a scoop net and a push or drag net. Both feature solid, long handles and a strong frame so that they can be pushed or dragged through the weed without bending. The net used is relatively fine and should be a strong mesh of 6–10 millimetres.

The best way to transport and keep mudeyes on a collection day or during a fishing trip is in an Esky as they must be kept in cool and dark conditions. The small six-pack esky is ideal for storing up to 100 mudeyes.

For long term storage mudeyes must be kept cool and in perfect darkness, otherwise they will hatch into dragonflies, so the fridge can be used. But they must be stored correctly; if they are immersed in water or are get too cold they will die. Use a polystyrene six pack Esky and place a layer of damp foam rubber on the bottom and put a layer of mudeyes on top. Another piece of damp foam is then softly placed on top followed by another layer of mudeyes. Continue this procedure until the Esky is full. Set the fridge on its lowest level. The mudeyes will then go into hibernation and will last for around four months.

Some mortality will occur during this period but expect a 70% survival rate; in warm weather there is no better alternative.

The other popular method of storage is to place water in a large Esky under the house. You will need 8 L of water per dozen mudeyes, and it needs to be changed every 10–14 days. Generally it is difficult to

Baitfishing from shore around flooded timber is always highly productive.

keep mudeyes alive for longer than 2 months this way.

Other hints include popping a few ice cubes into the six-pack Esky on hot fishing days to keep the mudeyes cool. Hot water promotes their metamorphosis into dragonflies and will cause them to become lethargic as they change.

In Australia, especially in southern waters, the mudeye is one of the most effective ways to entice big trout. The secret is to ensure that the mudeye is as lively and as natural as possible in the water. This is achieved by using a very small trout hook and hooking the mudeye through the base of the wings.

Finally and most importantly, be careful with fly repellent sprays and suntan creams. The tiniest amount of spray will kill your supply of mudeyes-their susceptibility to the slightest trace of insecticides cannot be over-emphasised.

Mudeye trolling

Trolling mudeyes behind Ford Fender or Cowbell attractors has to be one of the most consistent way of catching trout. But to be successful you need to do it perfectly, near enough is NOT good enough with this technique.

Boat speed should be dead slow (about 1 knot or less) so that the blades of the attractors are just turning properly. This gives the mudeye a darting motion, much like a free swimming insect. The trace behind the attractor should be as close as 16 cm when the trout are undoubtedly feeding or as far as a metre when the water is very clear or the trout are shy.

Troll two rods—where legal, check your local regulations—the first on a downrigger, back about 15 m and at the depth the fish are showing on the depth sounder; the other about 40 m back either with no weight or a ball sinker on the front of the attractor if the rig is to run lower in the water. The most important aspect of mudeye trolling is to take the time and care to properly mount the mudeye on the hook. A long shank, round bend, fine gauge, wide gape fly hook is used with a length to suit the size mudeyes you have available. The point is inserted right into the mouth and then pushed down the alimentary canal of the insect, carefully threading the mudeye around the shank of the hook. The point of the hook comes out exactly dead centre in the lower abdomen. You then very gently pull the hook so that the eye and the knot are pulled into the mudeye's head. Cut off the insects mandibles as they can cause the bait to spin.

When rigged like this the mudeye is pulled from the eye and line knot towards the front and does not spin. Check that it has not slipped back—often.

Cockroaches

Big, fat, shiny cockroaches are often found beneath dead logs and are excellent trout bait that can be fished either on the surface or under a float.

Grasshoppers and Crickets

When food is scarce trout are not very choosy about what insects they eat. However, over the summer months when grasshoppers and crickets are about in plague proportions trout can become quite selective and actively seek out these insects, making them one of the successful baits for trout. They can be remarkably effective in rivers and streams, as well as the windward shallows of lakes.

The traditional bait of many a small stream angler is simply to thread a grasshopper onto a hook tied directly to the end of his line. No weight or float is required in these small streams and the grasshopper is simply cast out and allowed to float naturally down the

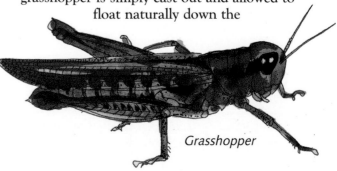

Grasshopper

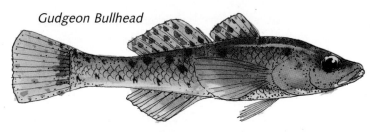
Gudgeon Bullhead

current. It is retrieved only when the insect drags across the water.

Many anglers do not realise that crickets and grasshoppers can also be effective when fished below the surface. This is because the number of submerged insects is often greater than those floating on the surface; this often suits the trout, as they will easily feed on these submerged terrestrial insects.

At times grasshoppers drifted in mid-water or along a stream bottom can catch many more trout than insects floated along the surface.

It is also effective to free-line the live grasshopper or cricket downstream on greased fishing line. A small split-shot is sometimes used to fish a submerged insect.

During summer a good source of crickets is the local tennis club. The lights on warm nights attract these insects and they can easily be collected. Alternatively, they can be flushed out of cracks in the ground during the daytime or found in amongst the building materials on suburban house building sites. Grasshoppers are best collected out in the fields in early morning when the coolness makes them lethargic and easier to catch.

Both grasshoppers and crickets can be kept for long periods in a well-ventilated cardboard box full of grass. Keep it in a cool place and they will stay alive for many weeks.

Minnows, Galaxiids and Gudgeons-live

In Australia the word 'minnow' means a small fish used for bait and covers galaxiids, jollytails, smelt, hardyheads, and gudgeons. All make good baits and do not even have to match the trout's natural diet to be effective.

The use of any fish as live bait in NSW is illegal. In Victoria it is illegal to use declared noxious fish in all waters. In some waters it is illegal to use redfin. If you do not know them, check the local regulations whatever State you are in before using fish as live bait.

Galaxiids (10–100 mm) form the largest family of fish in our cool southern waters. These are the main baits available in Victoria and Tasmania. Jollytails, a larger galaxiid (up to 160 mm) overlap into the warmer Murray/Darling system and form part of the diet of Murray cod and other bigger species. Gudgeons form the main block of species in NSW and southern Queensland. Combine these with smelt, small tench, roach and redfin and there is quite a large range of minnows available for bait.

The best way to procure live minnows is by trapping. There are many commercially available bait traps on the market using the 'wire drum' and

'one-way funnel' system. The collapsible shrimp box is a very good trap for most minnows.

Other methods of netting bait include drag netting and cast netting-you need to check whether they are legal in your particular State. Dip netting around weeds and other means of cover can, at times, produce bait. The best time to dip net is at night when the schools of baitfish are not as skittish.

When using live minnows keep in mind the size of the trout that you are seeking. A 500 g trout in a stream will ignore a 130 mm galaxiid. Also, most game fish prefer thin baitfish, as deep-bodied fish are difficult to swallow and can lodge in the fish's mouth, so keep the baitfish small.

Live minnows can be hooked in a number of ways:

Galaxiid
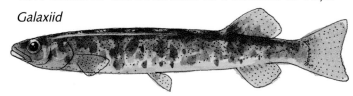

through the upper jaw
above the lateral line—just behind the shoulder—
through the base of the tail.

This last way of hooking galaxiids is particularly effective when hooking a pair of baits. Each excites the other, doubling the action and predator attracting vibrations.

Most often these baits are best suspended under a bubble or quill float. There are times when a free-swimming bait is more effective—especially when out in deep water. If more depth is required then split shot should be judiciously added. Again, remember the golden rule and always keep line size down to allow the bait to swim naturally.

Angling for baitfish with rod and line is also productive and very enjoyable. Light line, tiny hooks and good bait (corn, bread, small pieces of worms and larvae) are required, but even so they can be more difficult to catch than the target trout!

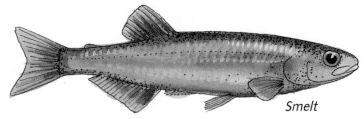
Smelt

Finally only catch live bait from the waterway in which you are going fishing. Don't translocate fish from one water to another.

Minnows and Whitebait—dead

A dead minnow is also a bait that is quite effective. The minnows should be fresh and presented as naturally as possible. Sew the line along the minnow starting at the head and up with the hook at the base of the tail. The bait can then be cast and retrieved in a natural manner.

A couple of other baits should be added to this section. They are whitebait and glassies—both of saltwater origin—and both have proved particularly effective in a lot of freshwater lakes in Victoria on rainbow trout and chinook salmon. At times, these saltwater baits have also been effective in Lake Hume and other NSW lakes. They can be fished on the bottom with some berley cast into the surrounding area or they can be trolled on a downrigger behind a dropper.

Mussels, Jap Clams and Pipis

These baits are surprisingly successful on trout. They rely heavily on the scent and juices they dissipate to attract trout.

The advantages of using them are that they are easily available, relatively cheap and can be kept for long periods of time in the freezer. They are predominantly saltwater in origin, however there is a freshwater mussel found in the Murray/Darling system that is a top bait for trout.

Shrimp

Hand nets of very fin mesh work well for catching shrimp in weeds and around shaded areas in our trout rivers and dams. Another popular method is to sink a shrimp trap (either an umbrella net or minnow trap) baited with meat, dead carp or Velvet Soap overnight. If no trap is available then a 'willow set' is a good standby. This is simply a big bunch of willow limbs 1.5–3.0 m long. These are placed into the water at the river's edge and left overnight or for several days. The shrimp are attracted to the mass of leaves.

Keeping shrimp alive requires many of the techniques outlined for live bait fish.

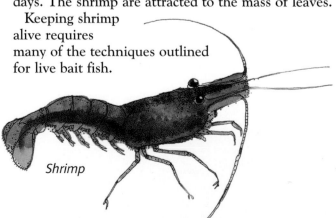

Shrimp

Brown trout in flooded rivers move to the edge. Scrubworms are a perfect bait in this situation as while the water is dirty the trout are often very active and will take a bait freely.

However, unlike fish, crustaceans can obtain oxygen from air, but only if their gills are wet. Consequently they can be kept in well aerated live bait tanks or in wet newspaper, hessian or weeds. They must also be kept cool—an insulated cool-box is ideal. Cool, dry sawdust will keep shrimp fresh, but not alive.

Shrimp are usually hooked tail-first and are always used live if possible. They can be rigged with a small, running ball sinker to get them down near the bottom, or under a quill, waggler or bubble float. The great success of shrimp is due to their scent. Trout seem to be able to detect the scent of a shrimp from a relatively long distance.

Being a soft bait, they require some special hooking techniques. This is especially so when using fresh but dead baits. They must be hooked through the tougher parts of their body or use a long shank hook and feed it right through from head to tail.

Slugs, snails and leeches

These are interesting and unusual baits. They will catch fish and are handy when nothing else can be found.

Ideally suited to small fish, they are often employed to fish for live minnows, and are excellent for ground bait or berleying.

Worms

Red Wriggles

Forget your lures and flies. More trout are caught on the humble worm than on all the other methods combined. This statement of fact may draw disapproval from some anglers as it conjures up visions of a forked stick and a bunch of worms anchored to the bottom. But there is much more to worm fishing than the sedentary approach.

Worms are a natural bait of the trout. When heavy rains and the snow melt occur in early spring, most trout anglers just stay indoors thinking of the season still to come.

But many experienced anglers dig some worms and head for the nearest trout stream. Trout feed heavily when the rising water dislodges worms from the banks, or flushes them out as rising lake waters cover new ground.

It often doesn't matter that the water is a bit discoloured—the fish will be actively pursuing the baits washed in. The best time to take advantage of this situation is during the first few weeks of a flood or rising water, although works will work exceptionally well all year round.

There are many species of worms in Australia and most prefer to live in rich loam soil. Whilst it is easy to classify worms into the two main headings of earthworms and scrub worms, in actual fact there are many sub-species of worms here, all inhabiting their own ecosystems and each requiring certain soil types and temperature range.

An earthworm eats its way through the soil, consuming its own weight in organic material every day! Worms do not have ears or eyes and are extremely sensitive to light, which is why they are rarely found above ground during the day.

Most species are found in moist earth and can be dug from gardens or beneath compost heaps. While the common garden worm is easily gathered, there are lots of other types that are much harder to find.

Scrub worms are usually bigger and often tougher than the garden worm and are a fantastic bait. There are many different types of scrub worms all around

Garden Worms

Australia. In the Dandenongs and around Healesville (Victoria) the scrub worm is a tough, medium sized worm that can be dug from the black loam around the banks of creeks. They are available for sale in the Melbourne tackle shops and are good bait for all freshwater species everywhere.

In the temperate rain forests of the Victorian Alps there is another type of scrub worm which is particularly good bait. It also likes the tussocky, moist loam around the banks of small creeks, particularly under the spreading foliage at the streamside. These fawn coloured scrubbies are up to 20 cm long and are as tough as nails with a wiry, leathery body. Trout in the streams just love them, and they are tough enough to take several trout on one bait. Even an inch of worm will take trout in the small streams and it would appear that they have a flavour that the trout can't resist.

In the Snowy high country there is another very large scrub worm that grows up to 25 centimetres. This creamy red worm is usually gathered by either turning over the debris at the edge of the lake when the water is rising, or by digging in the moist gullies around and under fallen timber and tussocks of grass. The trout feed on these big scrubbies when the water is rising and the trout will come right into the shallow water to feed on this bounty.

Along the Murray River the native scrub worm is much smaller and can be easily gathered around the edges of the lagoons. These worms must exude a sticky fluid, which must have a characteristic odour, that the fish find attractive.

These are but few of the many varieties used by anglers around Victoria and New South Wales. There are many more. Most worms are gathered by digging. Remember not to leave it too late in the season to collect your worms as once the ground gets hard and dry nearly all are difficult to find.

Keeping worms alive is easy as long as you keep them cool-neither too hot nor too cold. An old concrete trough or plastic drum can be filled with moist loam with vegetable scraps and old newspapers on the surface. As long as this is kept moist and cool the worms will stay and breed, giving you your own worm-farm and a constant supply of worms. Compost is also good to keep the worms in but it must be very well decomposed or the heat generated will kill the worms. Usually tiger worms do better in compost and earthworms in rich moist soil. If they get hot the worms will either migrate out of the tank or die.

The worms that are sold in plastic tubs are usually tiger worms. These small, banded worms are very lively, wiggling energetically and extrude a yellow liquid. At times they can prove effective on small fish.

Scrub Worm

Good quality worms will catch fish anywhere but local worms are usually the best. You can improve the imported worms by placing them in local soil, which brings their scent closer to the local variety.

While you are fishing worms are best kept in an ice-cream container with a few air holes in the top. This is kept in the Esky, but not right on top of the ice as they can freeze and die. In the high country do not leave them out overnight if there is any possibility of the worms freezing.

The methods used to fish worms are many. They can be trolled behind Ford Fenders or cowbells, anchored to the bottom with running or fixed sinkers, suspended under floats, allowed to drift with little or no weight in streams and cast without weight into lakes to await a trout.

Another important use of worms is as a sweetener on the hooks of lures. This is often enough to to tempt the trout into striking when the lure alone would be ignored.

Smaller worms are often best for trout, especially when bounced along the bottom of small streams and rivers. The rig to use in this situation is simple; just a small split-shot crimped directly onto the line about 60 cm above the hook. Cast upstream and allow the worm to tumble back with the current.

Mounting them on a hook depends on how you are going to fish the worms. Large scrubbies are best used alone, threaded onto the line to look like a worm that is drifting naturally. With the smaller earthworms, it is best to use a small bunch with each worm threaded twice onto the hook leaving plenty of ends to wriggle free.

Yabbies

In Dartmouth, Eildon, Eucumbene, Jindabyne and other large mainland Australian dams, the yabby—*Cherax destructor*—has become a major food source.

A look at the stomach contents of any big trout in these dams will reveal that they get big by

When baitfishing from the bank a long net handle can facilitate easy landing of your trout.

feeding on yabbies. Whether they prefer yabbies to other food is a point. However, in most cases they have no choice as big fish have big appetites—if there are no minnow schools to prey upon, the trout end up bottom grubbing for yabbies.

A classic example is Lake Dartmouth where the big trout feed deep amongst the snags almost all year round. They just don't have much in the way of alternative food sources. The problem for anglers is that while the trout are down there they are very difficult to catch.

The best places to find yabbies varies from place to place around the country, but try small farm dams, creeks, irrigation channels or lagoons. However, if pressed, by all means try directly in the rivers.

Remember that the excessively cold weather of winter cools the water and makes the yabbies go down to their holes and hibernate, or at least be very much less active. Consequently they are much more difficult to catch in the cooler months. There are a number of methods used to catch yabbies. The kids' method of a string with a lump of meat attached has been responsible for many good catches, but for quantities, a drag or scoop net pulled through the lagoons will result in bigger catches. The plastic shrimp net referred to earlier will also trap yabbies. The best method is to use a round hoop net or the black mesh yabby trap; both are sold in tackle shops.

Yabbies can be kept for months at a time as long as the water is not too warm. They are best kept in foam fish boxes with a firm-fitting lid as they can crawl out of just about any uncovered container. Have just enough water to not quite cover their backs. Sometimes they can start to try to burrow out of these boxes and can dig into the surface of the foam, but rarely get right through. Don't feed them meat and be sure to remove dead yabbies as you get increased mortality rates if the water is contaminated with putrefying material. Carrot rings or grated carrots are a great food and

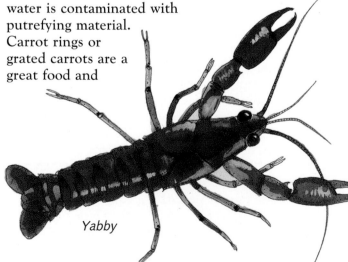

Yabby

Baitfishing from a boat allows for deeper presentations.

the yabbies thrive on it. Also remember not to put other baits in with the yabbies as they will make a meal of them.

Most anglers overlook the tiny 1–2 cm long yabbies, yet these are most likely the best size for trout. The methods for fishing these tiny yabbies are exactly the same as for mudeyes under floats. They can also be trolled behind ford fenders or dodger chains.

The slightly bigger yabbies can be fished in a number of ways. In shallow bays (2–3 m) one can float fish the yabbies just off the bottom. The yabby should be just hooked through the tail. Another way is to simply cast it out without any weight, and ever-so-slowly retrieve the yabby across the bottom.

In lakes with a shale or sand bottom one of the best methods is to use a paternoster rig and drift along in the boat with the sinker dragging along the bottom. Hook the yabby through the tail so that it is pulled backwards like a yabby trying to escape.

Another method to use in lakes in deep water is simply to jig or bob a yabby down deep around snags. This is effective in summer when the fish are deep and actively feeding on yabbies.

In streams, small yabbies are a good bait to cast and drift along the bottom in runs and pools. A fluorescent line, greased so it will float, will allow one to keep track of the progress of the yabby. Only add minimal sinker weight. *Fred Jobson & Bill Classon*

Mudeye Fishing

Fine brown monofilament that has been treated with a product like Cortland Dab to make it float is favoured by many baitfishers using mudeyes.

The humble mudeye, the nymphal stage of the dragonfly, is one of our deadliest trout baits whether used on still or fast waters.

I had anchored the boat just over a good cast away from a large weed bed in shallow water, a prime area to catch early morning browns on the mudeye. Picking the liveliest, blackest couta mudeye from the small foam Esky in the soft light of dawn, I pinned him through the wings on a tiny number 12 chemically sharpened hook.

I was easily able to cast well out at a right angle to my anchored boat using the larger of the two hard plastic bubble floats painted in luminous green and filled about three quarters full of water. With the

second luminous green bubble float cast out from the opposite side of the boat and starting its large swing drift in search of a target, it was time to sit back and take in the beauty that every summer dawn brings.

Mornings and evenings are great times to fish mudeyes under a bubble float as the winds are usually light which give a nice slow-to-moderate drift that is ideal for this style of trout fishing. In our summer months it is difficult to catch trout during the day as they move out and down as the sun rises. One method we've found successful is to fish very early— well before dawn to just after—and to target the shallow areas around weed beds, in many cases only a metre or two deep.

Fishing Live Mudeyes

The art in using live mudeyes is to keep them alive and kicking. To do so use a fine gauge chemically sharpened dry fly hook in a size 10–12 depending on mudeye size. The mudeye is simply hooked through the wings (figure 1). This does not harm the mudeye or impair its ability to swim.

The other key to fishing live mudeye successfully is to always use an open bail arm on your reel so that when the trout takes the bait it will feel no resistance. To stop the line from coming off the spool prematurely use a coarse angling accessory called a Run Clip. The line is simply pinned under the arm of the Run Clip (figure 2) where it will release at the slightest tug. This works as a bite indicator and allows the line to flow freely off the reel.

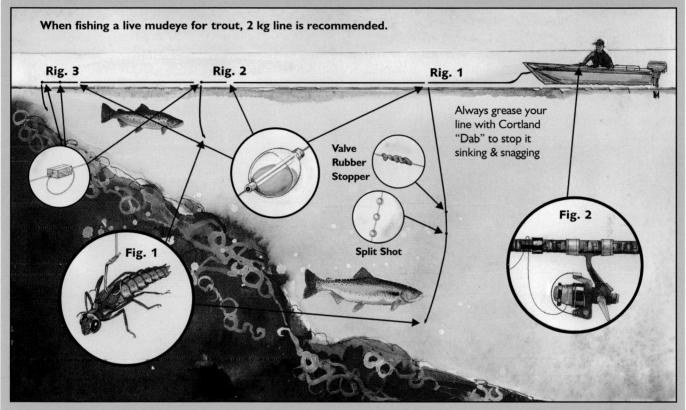

When fishing a live mudeye for trout, 2 kg line is recommended.

Rig. 3   Rig. 2   Rig. 1

Valve Rubber Stopper

Split Shot

Always grease your line with Cortland "Dab" to stop it sinking & snagging

Fig. 1

Fig. 2

Rig 1: This is a deep water rig where the mudeye can swim down pulling line through the bubble, the valve stopper will sink and not impede the mudeye's ability to swim. If fishing in windy conditions or if you want the mudeye to go deeper then simply add a split shot.

Rig 2: This is a fixed depth rig as the cork stopper floats and stops the mudeye going any deeper.

Rig 3: This rig is also fixed but uses two cork stopper floats. It is ideal for very shallow water where the trout are spooky. The second cork keeps the float well away from the swimming mudeye.

So it came as no surprise when the line came up tight after I flipped the bail arm closed to retrieve the rig so I could check the bait. Thinking it a small redfin, which came to the boat easily, I was stunned when I caught a glimpse of the fish's true size in my failing torchlight. With my heart in my mouth that split second I saw what I then believed was a brute of a 5 kg brown trout. Before this information had time to register firmly in my mind, the trout was making a blazing run against the drag back to the area it had left so easily only moments before.

Having had that fish of a lifetime so close then disappearing dangerously towards the weedbed I was anchored in front of, was a nerve-racking experience. Being by myself made it even more so as if I lost it, it would be a hard story for anyone else to swallow.

Fighting the urge to tighten the drag, all I could do was hold the rod high while the trout surged up and down the weedbed.

Slowly but surely it drew closer and closer, to within netting distance and capture. What a tug-of-war it was! It made this fish most memorable.

I weighed the large hen brown trout on a small set of scales. It fell short of my initial estimate but at 4 kg it was still the largest trout that I had been lucky enough to land to date.

The sun was over the horizon now but a welcome early morning fog was obstructing its growing intensity and allowed my productive fishing time to be increased. The two couta mudeyes had been resting in one position for some time and a recast would do no harm.

I watched one of the green bubble floats as it tracked past a large, partially submerged dead tree. It stopped dead in its tracks, drifted back against the wind then disappeared. Definitely a trout! The line was tumbling off the open bail.

This brown's fight was short but it hurtled out of the water four times and within two or three minutes was taken aboard.

It was a buck that went 3.3 kg on the lie detector. Truly unbelievable! Two trophies in one day and in January to boot!

When and where

These are definitely two of the most memorable fish I have had the pleasure to catch but looking back through my fishing diary they are not unusual. From early September right through to May each month, fishing mudeyes in the shallows in early morning, evening, heavy fog and overcast weather has produced amazing results in a variety of brown trout waters. There are waters all over Australia that are ideal for this early morning approach with mudeyes-refer to the fact box for details.

Just where to fish on an impoundment can seem difficult but if you think about it there are some basic concepts. A windblown shoreline, especially one with structure and weed beds, is a prime target. When the wind stops blowing be the first to fish it in the early morning or on evening as the wind dies. Apart from blowing food onto the shore, the cover of the chop can also spark trout activity, as they are more comfortable because of the increased camouflage.

Other hot spots are small openings amongst thick weedbeds, reedy areas or even partially sunken timber. These areas receive less attention from lake trollers.

Bubble float rigs

With the increased popularity of coarse angling in Australia there has been a move away from what is perceived to be the unsophisticated bubble float system. But the bubble float rig is one of the most effective and productive for trout in impoundments. It has many advantages. The main one is that it can be cast long distances without additional weight as the float itself, being partially filled with water, provides sufficient casting weight. In fact it is one of the easiest floats to adjust as both the casting weight

When bait fishing with mudeye under a bubble float have your rod setup parallel to the water.

and the height that it can float in water can be adjusted.

Bubble floats are available in a number of sizes, from a variety of manufacturers including the economical Dickson brand to the high-quality, higher-priced French brands. While there are a few different shapes made, the only one to use is the hard plastic, egg shaped model with the reasonably large hole through its centre. This allows your line to travel through unimpeded when a trout picks up and runs with the mudeye. A very handy model is the luminous green bubble float sold under the Dickson brand. I have found, after using several different colour combinations that it shows up best under most light conditions. To fill a bubble with water the central tube can be snapped out to let water in. Fill the float half to three quarters full, though its size and the distance to cast must be taken into account.

The whole key to fishing live mudeyes is to allow the trout to pick up the bait and run with it without feeling any weight. With a bubble float rig using light line (3 kg maximum) an open bail arm on a threadline reel and a bubble that allows the free passage of line then you have a system that allows just that! Ensure that the line doesn't prematurely spring off the reel by using a Run Clip to ever-so-lightly pin the line against the fore grip.

Another key to successful live mudeye fishing is to use light gauge, sharp hooks and the very best to use nowadays are chemically sharpened dry fly hooks in sizes 10–14.

The reason one uses a small hook is that the mudeye need only be hooked lightly through the wings. A light hook allows it to stay alive and still swim naturally.

The rig itself is relatively simple and involves passing the line through the float and attaching a stopper and the hook. No leaders are required and most successful anglers use 2 kg line straight to the hook. A small piece of cork with a slit in it is used for a stopper when one wants to exactly regulate the depth that the mudeye can swim to. If you are fishing over deeper water then use a valve rubber stopper. This will itself sink and allow the mudeye to swim down to a considerable depth. If an even greater depth is required, add a split shot, but only as a last resort.

The less weight on the line when fishing live mudeyes the better. Should you need to stop the line from sinking and snagging on the bottom or in weeds, use monofilament that floats to lessen drag when a trout takes the bait. Another key is to grease your line to stop it sinking—products like Cortland Dub are ideal for this purpose.

By far the best way to hook a mudeye is with a size 12 fly hook through the wings.

Anchoring

Anchoring the boat is probably as important as anything already mentioned. Position is the key factor. If the boat isn't in an ideal place to allow your bubble float to pass trout holding cover or territory it could be a waste of time. Take some extra time to locate yourself and if not completely satisfied, move, don't just sit it out.

If your boat is in very shallow water the best approach is to gently lower the anchor over the bow and to hold the chain clear while lowering it to reduce the noise. Alternatively a couple of simple steel weights can be used as anchors in shallow water-one for the bow and one for the stern—the ability to stop the boat from swinging is very helpful with a couple of anglers fishing multiple rods. *Wayne Tempest*

Baitdrifting

This trout was taken bait drifting on scrubworms around the shallows of Purrumbete.

Baitdrifting has suffered a decline in popularity compared with other techniques such as trolling, lurecasting, and static baitfishing. A pity as it is easily the most effective method of catching trout in rivers and streams.

Anglers who are able to anticipate the movement of trout and predict their behaviour are inevitably the most successful fishermen.

Such 'fish sense' has nothing to do with intuition. It is acquired through a knowledge of trout anatomy (particularly the sensory system) and an understanding of how fish respond to environmental changes to accommodate their four basic needs of comfort, self-preservation, food and procreation.

Most anglers are aware that the strongest and most aggressive trout take up the most favourable spots in a stream. In ideal conditions, these bossy fish fight off competition before locating themselves to one side at the head of a pool, a little below rapids and in close proximity to cover. From that spot they are able to hold their position without much effort; accept the benefits of fresh, highly oxygenated water that

tumbles into the pool; have first option on any dislodged nymphs that are swept out of the rapids; and quickly relocate to a safe refuge should the threatening shadow of a cormorant suddenly appear on the water.

With this fundamental knowledge of streamcraft, a wading angler has a good idea as to where to search for the biggest trout.

However, environmental variables such as the time of day, the time of year, the weather, the presence or absence of predators, the condition of the stream and the availability of protective cover can change trout behaviour in ways that would provide material for a hundred different scenarios.

There is no doubt that the acquisition of 'fish sense' is best drawn from a balance of bankside experience and appropriate reading.

When it comes to the vicarious learning of streamcraft and trout behaviour through books, articles and discussions, all the anglers are on a level plane. However in the school of practical experience the casters of artificials are greatly disadvantaged when compared to those who use live baits.

As one who enjoys all forms of angling, I appreciate the exhilaration experienced when a trout bows the rod as it chomps on a lure or gives notice of an impending battle as it slurps a fly from the surface of a stream. To take trout, either way, in the knowledge that your quarry has been seduced by nothing other than visual appeal, engenders a profound feeling of accomplishment.

But baitdrifting utilises all the trout's senses which, along with the virtues of its rigs and techniques, provide the exponents of this discipline with the potential to thoroughly exploit the weaknesses in a trout's defences and explore tight locations where artificial exponents dare not cast. As a result, it is not only the most prolific method of catching trout but it is the most proficient way of acquiring the knowledge that constitutes 'fish sense'.

Furthermore, the use of baits that necessitates the collection of wide variety of terrestrial and aquatic organisms, such as grasshoppers and crickets and the larval, nymphal and adult stages of caddis, mayfly, dobson fly, stonefly, damselfly and dragonfly as well as baitfish, mussels, snails, worms, leeches and cockroaches, engenders a fascination for zoology and entomology that remains for life.

Importantly though, the knowledge of streamcraft and trout behaviour and zoology and entomology that is acquired through baitdrifting is transferable and appropriate to the disciplines of fly fishing and lurecasting.

Very simply, baitdrifting involves an upstream cast of an unweighted bait that allows it to drift back to the angler through the movement of the current. In its basic form it is extraordinarily simple and unbelievably efficient.

Thirty years ago it was a method of fishing that was utilised by close to a third of the anglers one met along the banks of north-eastern Victorian streams. Nowadays, baitdrifting seems to be a forgotten art.

Gear

The casual or irregular baitdrifter will be able to practise this form of angling with a spinning rod and a small eggbeater reel but his selection of baits will be limited to only the heaviest such as scrub worm, grubs, cicadas and large 'couta mudeye' and yabbies.

The dedicated baitdrifter who intends to derive the benefits of angling light baits such as March flies, grasshoppers and tiny nymphs and larvae will need to employ a fly rod, fly reel and a light, stiff, monofilament line. However the new long spool threadlines and jigflicking rods will make a fist of casting light baits.

Catching and keeping aquatic baits

The collecting of baits can be as intriguing and as satisfying as catching trout. Very often, my mates and I spend much more time than is necessary exploring the bed of a river just to catch a larger nymph or to confirm the presence of a particular larva. From such undertakings so much can be learned about the location, movement and life cycles of aquatic creatures.

Even when I'm fly fishing, I often evaluate the bed of a stream that I intend to angle by checking out the variety, size, colour and stage of nymphs and larvae that are inhabiting the water in order to enhance my fly selection.

The most common aquatic insects to be taken from the bed of alpine streams are the nymphs and larvae of dragonflies, damsel flies, stoneflies, mayflies, caddis flies and Dobson flies. To facilitate their capture, a tennis racquet frame, with a fine mesh sewn into its face, becomes a most useful implement. Shallow runs, up to about 45 cm deep, prove to be the most manageable. By placing the net in the stream and dislodging the rocks immediately above it, the nymphs and larvae are swept into the mesh.

While this exercise is in progress the creatures that are caught can be kept together in a large plastic medicine jar. After the bait search has concluded, the larger nymphs such as mudeye and the bigger larvae like those of the dobson fly should be transferred to a 'six pack stubbie cooler' with a little water and some damp hessian. The smaller nymphs and larvae of stoneflies, caddis and mayflies can be kept in cool water in plastic phials. The water that sustains these creatures should be changed regularly to maintain the availability of oxygen.

When netting a river for bait it is advantageous to test a broad expanse of water that stretches from the bank to the centre of the stream in order to enhance the opportunity of snaring a variety of creatures.

When implementing the above processes it is not uncommon to turn up leeches, snails, freshwater mussels, yabbies, marron or an occasional shrimp, all of which can be used as bait.

Catching and keeping terrestrial baits

Terrestrial creatures that trout favour as food include worms, grasshoppers and crickets.

Worms

When searching for worms it is well to remember that these creatures consume large amounts of protein and cellulose, prefer soil that is barely damp and require ground temperatures to be 5–25°C in order to survive. As a result they can be very often found under logs, 'cow-pads', and humus that provide insulation and ample quantities of protein and cellulose. Red worms and 'scrubbies' are most favoured. Tiger worms are totally rejected by rainbow trout and are rarely taken by browns except in turbid water. Most worms that die after being caught do so because the soil in which they have been placed is too wet or too dry or temperatures to which they have been exposed exceed their acceptable limits.

Grasshoppers

Grasshoppers are sun-loving insects that become very active and difficult to catch during the heat of the day. They are best nabbed early in the morning while the dew is still about and before the sun warms the ground. It is important that they be kept in a clear plastic container, which has ample ventilation. The transparent container allows for a more even distribution of light which inhibits the hoppers' inclination to jump out the second the lid is lifted. Ventilation holes are needed to provide a constant supply of fresh oxygen, which is absorbed through spiracles in the insect's abdomen.

Crickets

Crickets are predominantly nocturnal by nature. Very often, they can be caught in urban areas beneath streetlights on warm evenings. In the country, they regularly locate themselves beneath dry 'cow-pies' and logs. A well-ventilated bucket with a lid makes an ideal keeper for these insects. The bucket should be stuffed with crumpled newspaper to provide the creatures with food and cover which inhibits their tendency to become cannibalistic when placed in a confined space. Crickets are probably the best, universally available, trout bait.

Beetles

In the fly fishing field, I am becoming increasingly convinced that beetle patterns are the most consistent takers of trout throughout Australia. As live bait, a Christmas beetle that is left struggling on the surface of a backwater is a temptation that trout are rarely able to resist. These creatures are tough and resilient and can be kept for long periods in a matchbox or similar container.

Moths

Larger, bulkier moths such as the Bogong moth that are easily cast also attract trout well.

Grubs

Wood grubs, which are the larvae of beetles and moths, also readily draw trout attention but ground grubs appear to be much less appetising. Wood grubs can be purchased at a number of fishing tackle outlets or procured through a half-hour effort in the wood-heap. They keep well in cool, dry sawdust.

Cicadas

Cicadas, because of their inept capacity to fly, often end up falling into a stream from where they are easily captured and used immediately. Their bulkiness, which enables them to be cast long distances, is most useful in clear water where anglers need to take care not to be spotted by wary fish.

Cockroaches

Cockroaches, that can be located beneath logs around the perimeter of lakes, are a popular bait in Western Australia and proved to be very productive during a recent fishing trip to the west.

Blowfly larvae

Blowfly larvae (maggots or gentles) have become increasingly popular in recent years and their value as bait is indisputable. They can be grown on flesh cultures and then kept in dry bran or sawdust until needed, or they can be purchased from various fishing tackle shops.

Crustaceans

The yabby is an excellent bait for most native fish and redfin but it is less productive in the trout fishing stakes. However it is interesting to note that Western Australian trout are particularly partial to young marron.

It is illegal to use frogs and tadpoles as bait but it should be mentioned that artificials that emulate the movement of these creatures take a lot of fish late in the evening and during the night.

Hooking baits

The potential to catch fish when baitdrifting is partially determined by the distance of a cast and the quality of the natural drift of the bait. The bigger the hook the greater the potential to cast further but the greater the imposition on the natural drift. As a result, the selection of hook size is always a compromise between these two factors. A rule of thumb is to use the largest hook possible to 'naturally' accommodate the bait that is being used at a particular time.

One of the classic examples of the need to use different hooks for different applications evolves out of the presentation of live crickets. By using a size 2 silver suicide hook, the average cricket will drift to the bed of a river to entice the bottom feeders that are in residence. However, by employing light size 8 hook the same cricket will float and swim on the surface of the water and attract upper level fish.

While fly-fishermen and lure-casters can hope to draw a trout's attention through the visual attractiveness of their presentation alone, a baitdrifter

Baitdrifting Techniques

THE CONVENTIONAL RIG

The conventional rig for baitdrifting comprises a size 4 hook attached to a 2 kg monofilament line.

THE CONVENTIONAL RIG WITH BAIT SHANDY

A conventional rig with a size 2–4 hook and a worm threaded onto the shank provides sufficient weight to cast even the lightest baits.

THE DUAL LEADER RIG

The dual leader rig comprises a brass ring from which a short leader and a long leader are tied. The short leader has a size 1–4 hook attached while the long leader has a size 8–12 hook tied. The bigger hook is used to hold a heavy bait to provide the mass needed to cast while the smaller hook is used to present a lighter bait.

The 'flicking' rig comprises a 1–2 kg line to which is attached a size 4–6 long-shanked keeper hook. The mudeye is impaled through the front of the thorax and the hook is drawn along the abdomen to exit through the rear orifice. Used in sluggish or still water, it is cast and then retrieved in jerky movements to simulate the natural swimming action of the nymph. As a method that consistently takes trout there is none better.

The hooking of three grasshoppers provides additional mass, which leads to easier casting. The first two are threaded from 'head to toe' and exude plenty of bodily fluids that spread through the water and attract trout through their sense of smell. The last one, which is barely nipped through the thorax, provides the movement, which helps to attract the fish visually.

FLAT WINE WARP RIG

This rig utilises a size 2–4 hook with a 1.5 cm square of lead-like wine bottle wrap. This wrap provides the weight necessary to cast a single March fly or any other light bait. The flat nature of the wrapping has a wing effect, which provides buoyancy in fast-moving water and helps to keep the bait drifting at around mid-stream level.

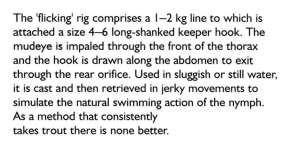

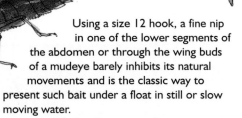

Using a size 12 hook, a fine nip in one of the lower segments of the abdomen or through the wing buds of a mudeye barely inhibits its natural movements and is the classic way to present such bait under a float in still or slow moving water.

It is important to ensure plenty of wriggling ends to draw a trout's attention and interest.

can exploit all the fish's senses through movement and smell and the authenticity of the taste and texture of the bait. If the bait is fresh, the fish, which has been attracted to it, will accept the taste and texture as authentic and palatable.

It has been my experience that baits that are presented on or near the surface need to be visually attractive and that deeper baits need to appeal to smell and taste.

When relying on mudeye to provide natural movement, it should be nipped in the wing-buds with a small hook. But if it is the intention of the angler to impart the movement into the mudeye, as is the case when using the 'flick and retrieve' method of presentation, the nymph needs to be threaded on to a long-shanked keeper hook by entering the barb in the thorax and exiting through the rectum.

Nipping a yabby to one side of the fifth tail segment allows it ample freedom of movement and a live galaxia or smelt that is hooked through the bottom lip will remain alive and active until it is taken by a hungry fish.

Rigs

The most common baitdrifting rig simply comprises a hook at the end of a line. In most cases the total weight of the hook and the bait provides sufficient terminal mass for the rig to be cast.

However when one is using light baits or is confronted by a stiff headwind the terminal mass of the rig often needs to be increased. This can be accomplished in a number of ways but my preference is to use a dual hook rig.

This rig involves the tying of a brass ring at the end of the line. To the ring, a short and a long leader are attached. The short leader utilises a large hook and a heavy bait while the longer leader makes use of a smaller hook and a smaller bait. This configuration enables the rig to be well cast without inhibiting the natural drift of the baits.

Streamcraft and tactics

Experienced anglers wade upstream and approach their quarry from behind whenever possible.

The position that a trout takes up in a stream is determined by its requirements, which revolve around needs for food, comfort and self-preservation and a drive to procreate.

By carefully observing the flow of water that is carrying food and noting the proximity of positions that afford comfort and protection, one will soon acquire a sound first-hand knowledge of where trout are likely to be located.

There are other variables, such as seasonal factors, the state of the water and the time of day along with attributes pertaining to a trout's sensory system and its capacity to be conditioned, that affect trout behaviour. The more one comes to appreciate these additional factors and turn them to one's own advantage the closer one comes to acquiring that elusive 'fish sense'.

Baitdrifting for trout works everywhere from big rivers to small creeks.

Casting

Anglers who choose to practise baitdrifting with a spinning reel and rod will be limited to the use of heavy baits such as worms, cicadas and large couta mudeye.

Those who use a fly rod and reel and 2–3 kg monofilament will be able to present a wider range of lighter baits.

When using the configuration, 6 or 7 m of line is stripped off the reel and held in the left hand. When the right arm pushes the rod forward to cast the left hand releases the line which slides through the runners much more easily than if it had been released from a reel.

It takes time and practice to perfect but it's worth it! Once the basic overhead cast has been mastered the need to use side casts and underhand casts becomes apparent as an angler discovers the necessity of reaching those difficult spots that harbour large trout beneath over-hanging bankside trees.

The drift and strike

Once the cast is complete and the bait hits the water the drift begins. How natural its movement in the current is will largely determine the response of a trout to the bait.

At this stage it should be the angler's aim to retrieve line, as the bait draws closer to him. Often the presence of a fish can only be detected when the line stutters in its movement.

When fishing an artificial in such circumstances, the strike would need to be employed immediately so that the fish has no chance to detect the false flavour and texture. However, when angling an authentic bait, which radiates a tantalising odour that is accompanied by a succulent flavour and appropriate texture, the fisherman should peel off some line to allow the trout to test the offering without inhibition. Usually, within a minute, the movement of the line at the surface of the water will indicate that the fish has accepted the bait. This is the time to strike.

Alternative approaches to baitdrifting steams

When one intends to present light baits such as adult damselflies and dragonflies that are wind-resistant and difficult to cast, a different approach needs to be employed.

Very often the only way such a bait can be presented is by fishing downstream.

The ideal position from which to do this is from beside a run, immediately upstream from a pool. By casting into the run and quickly feeding out line the dragonfly will drift downstream and into the pool where it will float on the surface to tempt any trout that happens to be in residence.

Tiny mayfly nymphs can be presented with a cross-stream cast. After feeding out ample line to allow downstream drift it will finally straighten and swing cross-stream back towards the angler before the nymph rises from the bed of the steam. It is at this point that a trout will very likely snatch at the bait.

What about lakes?

The first rule relating to lakes is to know which trout are in residence. Rainbows are taken more readily during daylight hours while browns are inclined to feed during the evening and into the night.

A receding lake is rarely worth fishing unless one can reach deep water such as the bed of an old river. But a rising lake is always full of promise when fished over freshly covered ground. When angling such shallows, an unweighted line, that is used to present heavy baits such as scrub worms and mussels that exude attractive odours, will most often draw the best response.

Beside weed beds, a mudeye that is nipped through the wing buds and presented below a float is a well proven method of taking trout' but the 'flick and retrieve' method of presenting a mudeye can be even more productive. This technique involves the threading of a mudeye on to a keeper hook before casting it over the reeds and retrieving with intermittent jerks.

Baitfish that are hooked through the lip with a size 6 or size 8 hook produce good results when angled a metre or so off the bottom in deep water.

At night, a cricket, which is presented on top of the water through the use of an unweighted line and a size 8 hook, can produce lots of action.

Conclusion

The challenge and the feeling of accomplishment involved in catching fish on lures and flies that rely entirely on visual presentation is indisputable.

However baitdrifting, which exploits all fish senses, provides not only the potential to catch more trout, but in doing so, furnishes a thinking angler with the opportunity to learn the elements of streamcraft and 'fish sense' much more effectively than his compatriots who use artificials.

*But for those who want to know everything including all disciplines, streamcraft, 'lake-craft', trout behaviour, traditional fallacies relating to trout and Australia wide locations, Bill James' book 'Catching Trout in Australia' which was released in October 1994 will provide most valuable reading. **Bill James***

Bubble Float Fishing

Fishing around weed beds it pays to suspend your bait under a bubble float to get best results.

The day is getting hotter and hotter and the gentle breeze has dropped to provide warm and still conditions, not ideal trout fishing weather at any impoundment.

In years gone by this would have heralded a change of plan, maybe pursuing redfin with bottom baits or a few hours spent trolling instead. But now we have another approach to catching trout in the heat of a day—deep water bait fishing. We use bubble floats to suspend an offering just off the lake floor or weed beds, enticing the fish that aren't going to rise dramatically in the water level to take it.

Fishing in 5 metres of water with straggly weed protruding up to half a metre off the bottom, we fish floats with baits down at 4.5 metres. They are barely above the carpet of weed and occasionally are fouled

Victorian Destinations

Lake Toolondo
The entire lake is excellent for deep water float fishing with its maze of sunken and partially sunken dead timber and large weed beds to fish towards or away from. The author's favourite areas are along the deep West Bank and out from Officers. A depth sounder will locate other trout producing hide-outs without too much trouble. Deep water fishing is a good method to use at any time at Lake Toolondo but when there is a lot of boat traffic zipping about on a weekend it is one of the best tactics to use.

Lake Fyans
This particular lake is fast gaining a reputation as one of Victoria's best

trophy brown and rainbow trout waters. It is where the author first used baits over 3 metres below a bubble float in calm weather conditions.
Drifting mudeyes or worms near partially submerged timber out from the main wall or near the inlet channel is a rewarding way to fish, as is tying up to timber. A depth sounder can locate some excellent spots between heavy weed growth - an anchor will be needed.

Cairn Curran Reservoir
There are definitely times at this popular reservoir when shallow to medium bait fishing is the best approach, especially with rising water levels. In low water

conditions or warm weather when trout seek out cooler regions it can be a different story. Concentrate efforts near the mouth of Treloars Bay, 2nd Wall, Main Wall and on the edges of the old river course. Although the methods outlined are targeted at trout don't be surprised if you hook a good-sized golden perch or redfin.

Lake Purrumbete
This extinct volcanic crater lake is very deep, dropping away steeply right from the shore's edge. Good fisherman and friend Rob Garner and I have had success fishing mudeyes and pieces of salted whitebait up to 6 metres below bubble floats at Lake Purrumbete.

We have landed brown trout to 2.4 kilos (a recent addition to the lake that are doing really well), chinook salmon close to 1.5 kg and several feisty catch and release rainbows.

Other Waters
Lake Murdeduke hasn't got an over abundance of really deep water but we have had good captures fishing a long way out from shore in 4 to 5 metres of water. Wartook Reservoir is well worth exploring and so is Rocklands Reservoir. I have no doubt there are a great many other lakes and reservoirs where a little trial and error would unlock some trophy sized trout hiding in the deep water.

by it on their super slow drifts. It is usually very easy to tell if they are fouled as the float stops drifting. Giving them a slight tug usually frees them but a few hooks and baits will be lost. If you aren't occasionally getting hooked up though, you are not fishing in the strike zone.

We cast as close as possible to some partially submerged dead gum trees (fish attracting structures) in front of us. With next to no drift the floats are near the trees for quite some time before slowly drifting away. The only bites we encounter are when our baits (spider mudeyes) are less than a metre from the partially submerged trees.

The bites are touchy—the cork goes down then pops back up several times before there's a steady take where a hook-up is possible. If we hadn't known better, we might have confused this action with having small redfin playing up in the area. But these fish aren't redfin, they are just cautious trout which, due to the weather conditions, don't want to stray too far from the safety of the weed and snags.

Using this method I have landed trout especially browns up to 3.8 kilos whereas other people have frequently given up in disgust.

Tactics and Rigs

Warm weather, with or without a breeze, provides excellent conditions for this type of fishing but it is also worth persisting with on other occasions - early mornings, late evenings, when it is windy or raining and during other weather conditions.

We fish this way in water 3 metres to 6 metres deep; it is no use fishing shallower when the fish are chasing a feed down deeper.

The most common rig for fishing at these depths is a bubble float set up (refer to diagram) or a straight-over-the-side approach. Bubble floats have been put on the backburner by a great many anglers who have found the European coarse fishing wagglers and stick floats more to their liking. They definitely have a place in all serious trout fishers' tackle boxes but with leaders up to 6 metres being used bubble floats have a distinct advantage. The majority of stick floats can't be cast great distances, or changed in seconds if the water is too deep or shallow and they are sometimes fixed on the line. If using a fixed float, the float can be at the rod tip and the fish nowhere near the net, causing havoc at the boat and sometimes disaster.

For shallow water my rig consists of a bubble float above a cork stopper with a slit cut into it. The line is then wrapped once over the incision to stop it slipping and changing the predetermined depth setting. A small number 12 chemically sharpened hook is tied on and a small split shot added halfway

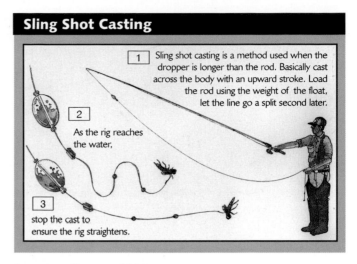

Sling Shot Casting

1   Sling shot casting is a method used when the dropper is longer than the rod. Basically cast across the body with an upward stroke. Load the rod using the weight of the float, let the line go a split second later.

2   As the rig reaches the water,

3   stop the cast to ensure the rig straightens.

between float and bait.

For deep water exactly the same rig can be used but the slit in the cork must be large enough to break and fall off once a large fish is encountered, otherwise the same problem occurs as when using fixed floats. By replacing the cork stop with a Styrofoam one an immediate clearance is made on hook-up as a rule.

Having two anglers aboard the boat we fish two rods each with bubble float distances and depths staggered. But at some of the best trout waters across the state there are partially submerged dead trees that make ideal places to tie up to and fish for trout. Once tied up it is worth casting floats towards or past other nearby snags. You can also try lowering a bait directly over the side of the vessel into the strike zone. Depending on the wind and chop on the lake's surface this can mean using just a few split shot

It pays to use longer rods when bubble float fishing—either from a boat or from the land.

Setup

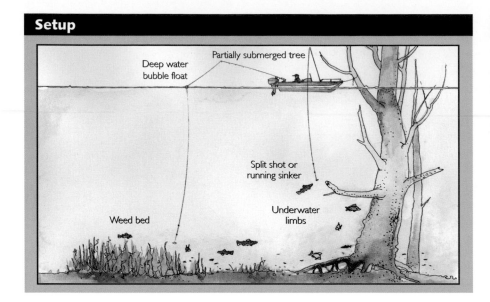

Deep Water Bubble Rig

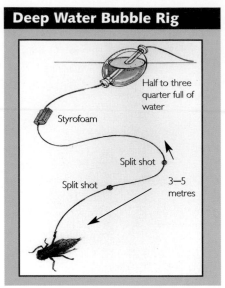

crimped above the bait or small running sinkers.

Let the bait down until it hits the lake floor, then wind it up half a metre or less so it is just clear. With the bait set and the rod placed in a holder, bites can be missed if the drag is left engaged. To overcome this we use a small rubber band around the forward grip of the rod. Placing just a bit of line under the rubber band, stops the bait plummeting down and when a trout goes to take the bait there is little resistance felt. Then it is just a matter of playing it cool until it is time to set the hook.

Best Baits

When it comes to baits for trout there are literally hundreds to experiment with so the following is just a guide to some of the more successful ones that are usually fairly easy to obtain at most times of year.

Mudeyes

Most trout will feed at one time or another on the mudeye, the nymphal stage of the dragonfly. Most frequently used is the couta mudeye but its small relation, the spider mudeye, is also an excellent

Bait fishing at anchor on Lake Purrumbete in Victoria. Notice how the rods are set up horizontal to the water. This aids bite detection and successful hook-ups.

choice. Looking at them side by side it is hard to understand why a trout would swim past a couta to take a spider mudeye but they are a more commonly occurring food source in many waters.

Worms

Worms are usually associated with bottom fishing and are used with running sinkers and large bunches on size 4 hooks but we have had success using them beneath bubble floats. Worms can catch trout all year around but seem to always fish best after heavy rains in September. Hook size (12) stays the same with two garden worms barely hooked on so they wiggle, strongly attracting fish. Scrub worms are bigger and call for a slightly larger hook so fish aren't missed: maybe go up to a size 10 or 8 chemically sharpened hook and only use one worm at a time.

Yabbies

When trout are actively chasing yabbies they can be hard to catch as they are feeding off the lake floor generally in low light conditions. I have had next to no luck using bottom baits at these times but suspending a tiny kicking yabby under a float has worked. Keep it really deep and remember, for best results, fish early morning or after sunset when the resident yabby population is on the move.

Salted Baits

Large salted glassies, blue bait and white bait are common salt water baits but in the last few years they have been recognized as red hot rainbow trout tempters. They hit it hard and take off like a bull seeing red but a lot are missed before hook up. Maybe the hook was buried in the glassies' flesh, or when it ran, water pressure on the line pulled the bait free. Sometimes I think the bait is just too big and hard to cover using one hook. Two hook rigs with the barbs well clear will do a little better with fewer missed strikes, that is, with bottom baits. However people have been slow to fish these under bubble float set ups as they are too large and you would have to use an extra big piece of cork to keep it afloat.

When fishing with these salted baits I berley by breaking up a salted bait into half a dozen pieces and scatter them around the fishing area. By putting one of the small parts on a number 8 hook results have been good with very few misses. It makes sense that if these trout are feeding on your berley they are going to take a similar sized piece hiding a hook without hesitation.

Casting

When using a mudeye rod around 2.7 metres long, I find short casts with droppers under this length are quite easy to accomplish. If long accurate casts are required fill the bubble float to three quarters of its capacity and feather the line as it draws close to hitting the water. Doing this will prevent the set up from landing in a big pile and drifting around in a terrible tangle. Once the float is on the water pull it a short distance back to straighten out any twists then flick out some slack for the float to get a good drift. Most of our bites are registered on the drift so don't wait too long to cast out again.

A longer dropper from 3 to 5 metres is very hard to cast. Some people will drop the float next to the boat then let it drift. I have seen others stand right up on the front of their boats or seats and have great difficulty trying to cast such long droppers below a bubble. If you use a sling shot method very few tangles will occur and only the odd bait is flicked off. Have the float centimetres below the rod tip and baited hook in hand. When the float is cast as normal the bait follows off the hand and a reasonable distance can be achieved. It will take some practice and be careful not to hook yourself or people standing close by. These lines will also need tethering before they hit the water, to stop tangles and to have the rig straighten out. *Wayne Tempest*

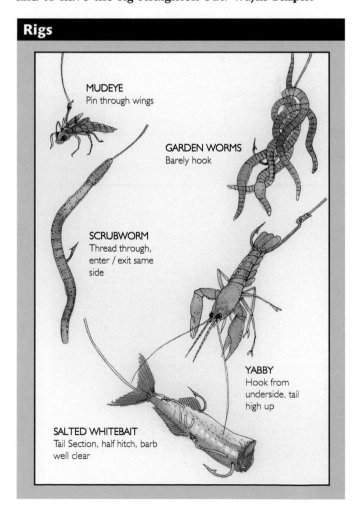

Rigs

MUDEYE
Pin through wings

GARDEN WORMS
Barely hook

SCRUBWORM
Thread through,
enter / exit same
side

YABBY
Hook from
underside, tail
high up

SALTED WHITEBAIT
Tail Section, half hitch, barb
well clear

Spinner blade lures

Spinners are a hot lure for trout in rivers and are often the first choice of experts.

Spinner blade lures are easily the most versatile of all freshwater lures for lure casting. They work on all waters from creeks to rivers to lakes and large impoundments. They can trigger an instant 'attack response' in trout in a small creek or fool big trout and salmon in our lakes into thinking it is a fleeing baitfish.

Unfortunately very few freshwater anglers understand the various styles of spinner blades, the reasons for their subtle variations in construction and most importantly the changes in retrieval methods needed to get the best and most desired action out of each type of spinner blade.

This chapter will open your eyes to the effective methods of spinner blade lure casting and just how to catch more fish using this group of lures.

Before going into the specific types of spinner blades there are some general points that should be noted. Contrary to popular belief, in general practice all spinner blades should be worked on the SLOW side. Quality spinner blades will rotate and work even at extremely low speeds. This makes them extremely effective on trout in very cold or very warm water when these salmonids are lethargic and not disposed to chase anything too fast.

So look to slowing down your retrieval rate when using spinner blades, even vary the rate. Remember that many spinner blades work very effectively when simply jigged over the stream bed of a river.

Have a good look at your spinner blades, and you will notice that the blade shapes differ. The bigger and broader the blade, the greater the water resistance and the greater the angle it rotates on the shaft. The Colorado blade is the broadest, and spinners with Colorado blades will run the shallowest for a given crank speed.

These wide blades are best in slow moving rivers and lakes where a slow to moderate speed is required together with plenty of thump and strong vibrations from the blade.

The smallest of the blades is the narrow Willow Leaf. Spinner blades with Willow Leaf blades are best for fast moving rivers and medium to fast retrieves. They also work well when jigged fast across the bottom as the Willow Leaf blade starts moving more quickly and easily than any other blade shape.

Shaft Spinners

Shaft spinners, standard spinners or just 'spinners' are one of the most popular and effective lure casting lures every produced.

They are probably the best lure for stream and river lure casting for trout. In fact, so popular is this lure that the term 'spinning' is synonymous with lure fishing for trout for many anglers.

Standard spinners though do have their limitations. As they are light and the spinning blade has the effect of planning them up to the surface, they are not the best choice for deep water. Additionally, they work best in open water and they are not weed resistant. Even small amounts of weed will kill the action of the finely balanced spinner.

Having said that, put them in their element—streams, creeks, shallow rivers, shallow bays of lakes and backwaters—and you will be hard pressed to find a more productive style of lure.

Types of Standard Spinners

There are two main styles of spinners. The main type attaches the blade to the shaft by a clevis pin. All blade shapes can be used in this configuration—Colorado, Indiana, French and Willow Leaf.

The other style is the Sonic-Blade spinner where the blade spins directly on the shaft. These blades are shaped so they are concave above their axis point and convex below it. This configuration allows almost instant spinning at extremely low retrieval rates. The speed of blade rotation is the fastest of any spinner blade (faster spin rates can be achieved than those obtained with a Willow Leaf on a clevis pin). Sonics are ideal for fast stream and river lure casting.

How to Retrieve Standard Spinners

In Australia, standard spinners would come close to being our top lure casting choice for trout. They can be dynamite on redfin and Atlantic salmon, effective for Macquarie perch and trout cod and are handy additions to your armoury for bass, golden perch, and chinook salmon.

The most effective size for river and stream work are spinners in the range 1" to 2" with Sonics or Willow Leaf or French blades best. In lakes, go up to 3" in length and look to Colorado or Indiana spoons.

As mentioned, spinners can be retrieved most effectively at times by jigging them across the bottom of a trout steam—cast them across stream and jig back across and up against the current. The art of jigging and spinning is not to do it too erratically, as the blade won't rotate as the spinner sinks. Your retrieval rate will determine the jigging style, not your rod.

Retrieving spinners at a constant speed often results in follows, but no takes; varying retrieval speeds imitate fleeing baitfish. Varying the speed of blade rotation changes the underwater vibration and causes the trout to sit up and take notice.

In lakes and slower waters, use heavier, longer spinners to get deeper. Choose big, wide blades to get maximum pulse and attraction. Again, don't retrieve at a constant rate—vary speed by varying retrieval rates.

Weight-forward Spinners

We now move into the other categories of spinners (including weight-forward spinners and spinner baits and buzzbaits).

Amazingly, these are the lost cousins here in Australia. Very few anglers understand their uses, the technology involved or the correct techniques involved to get the best out of them.

Weight-forward spinners feature an extended shaft with a lead weight head forward of the spinner blade and body. Like standard spinners, the blade shapes vary and again like standard spinners they are designed purely for lure casting.

The lead weight facilitates longer casts and gets the lure right down deep. Usually the body is the shape of a heel to help minimise line twist. This fast sinking design makes this variation of the spinner ideal for getting down deep in very fast rivers and in lakes and reservoirs. They are a great choice when you need to get the lure down to the bottom of a river and stay there.

How to Retrieve Weight-Forward Spinners

The first thing to mention about weight-forward spinners is that if they're cast out incorrectly, they will tangle every time! They require more of a 'lob' cast: if thrown out with a snap cast, the hook will often catch on the line. It is also handy to stop the lure just before it hits the water and control the sink. This will prevent the hook from fouling on the line as the lure sinks. Also as they have a built-in heel, don't use a snap swivel.

Tie the line directly to the eye of the lure. Snap swivels will only increase the amount of foul-ups during casting.

Having overcome these hurdles, the good part comes as these lures start working the instant they hit the water. Due to the positioning of the lead head, the lure sinks headfirst so the blade will spin on the drop.

To retrieve, use rod action and vary the retrieval rates of the reel to generate action. Long sweeps of the rod are better than short, sharp, jigging actions. In certain situations a constant retrieve can work, especially when using a countdown method to find the right strike zone depth.

The weight of these lures will keep them at the strike zone depth for a better part of a constant retrieve. *Bill Classon*

Plugs & Minnows

In some ways, this lure grouping is the 'messiest' and least definable of all, containing as it does such a wondrous diversity of hardware. Sub-groups within this class would have to include at least the following: minnows, plugs, bibless rattlers, sonics, prop baits, stick baits, chuggers, crawlers, sliders and poppers.

Actually, the Americans have a pretty good way of handling this classification problem. They call all these lures 'body baits'. In other words, they all have a reasonable robust and obvious 'body', which is usually made of plastic or wood. The term body bait separates them from jigs, spinners, spoons, soft

Trout minnows come in a myriad sizes and colours. They usually feature a tight shimmy action, even in a deeper diving configuration.

plastics and other lure classes.

Whether we call them plugs and minnows or body baits, there's no denying that this vast army of lures represents the largest grouping of artificials in freshwater angling. Because they are also the most variable in their performance and different in their ideal applications—not to mention most expensive— they can easily confuse the novice. Indeed, more than a few experienced fishermen have trouble in selecting a particular model, size and colour for a specific scenario.

History and evolution

Plugs and minnows started out as freshwater lures. In fact, they evolved primarily for catching the American largemouth bass. Those early plugs were 'whittled' from lumps of wood and were basically intended as surface or sub-surface representations of field mice, large insects or injured baitfish. Their origins date back to the early 1800s.

Later, the backyard whittlers began adding metal diving lips or 'bibs' to their crude creations. This caused them to dip beneath the surface when retrieved and in some instances, to swim or wobble in a manner appealing to predatory fish.

Some of the earliest American plugs, like the Bass-O-Reno, are collector's items today, and are cherished by older anglers in much the same way as the Aussie-made Bellbrooks, which emerged on the local scene after World War Two. There's little doubt that the advent of these Australian plugs was spawned by contact between fish-minded servicemen in places like New Guinea and North Africa, not to mention the Yanks who were stationed here is Australia during the war.

Interesting, a parallel if somewhat different evolutionary process was taking place in northern Europe, where commercial freshwater fishermen had begun carving baitfish imitations to catch trout, salmon and pike. These were loosely modelled on primitive ice fishing decoys—large fish shapes that were floated on or suspended through holes in the ice in order to lure fish close enough to be speared!

The first European fisherman to really refine his baitfish imitation and begin marketing it on a small, local scale was a Finn named Laurie Rapala. This was during the mid to late 1950s.

Laurie sent some of his early minnows to America, and they brained the Yank fish—not just bass, but many species which had taken less readily to the fat-bodied, American-style plugs. These included the likes of walleye, muskie, trout and salmon.

In 1962, a remarkable thing happened. An American journalist wrote a short item on Laurie Rapala's lures for 'Life' magazine. The editor sat on the feature for several weeks, but by a quirk of fate, the issue he decided to run it in was the one carrying news of Marilyn Monroe's controversial death. That edition of *Life,* complete with a provocative cover photo of the late blonde bombshell, smashed existing sales records. Overnight, the word 'Rapala' became a household name among America's millions of freshwater anglers.

Within weeks, Rapala minnows had become a precious commodity in North America. At a time when weekly incomes averaged $40 or $50, Rapala 'Originals' sold for $5 a pop, and some stores actually hired them out for weekends, with a $20 security deposit in case they were lost!

If the modern era of plugs and minnows can be said to have a starting date, then it was surely the date on which that edition of *Life* magazine hit the news stands.

The Australian scene

Australian anglers were quick to take to plugs and minnows. Early Bellbrooks, American imports and backyard products worked like a charm on our fish. Vic McCristal told me a yarn about being posted to Bourke, in outback NSW, during the late 1950s. Armed with his then state-of-the-art baitcaster gear and a plug carved from an old wooden clothes peg, he regularly accounted for cricket score catches of yellowbelly in the broken water below the town weir. It would be an understatement to say that the local setline and drum net merchants sat up and took notice!

Large minnows and floating divers have become popular and have accounted for many large trout.

The Rapalas and other European-style, thin-bodied minnows arrive a few years later, making their biggest impact on the northern barramundi scene and among saltwater lure casters targeting flathead and the like. They were also dynamite on trout. In our newly filled hydroelectric dams.

These early body baits were expensive, and in the typical Australian fashion, local craftsmen were soon copying the imports and modifying them for local conditions. This formed the basis of a cottage industry that would ultimately bloom in the 1980s, with Smith and McGrath coming to the forefront.

However, the 1960s and 1970s were dominated by imports. This was the age of the ABU Hi-Lo and Killer, the Rebels and Rebs, the Cotton Cordells, Rapalas and Nilsmasters, Heddons and Arbogasts. They were all good, but they were all expensive— very expensive. Newcomers bemoaning today's lure prices should stop for a moment to consider that we regularly paid $5 and more apiece for those imported lures—and that was at a time when the average working man took home between $100 and $150 a week! On a relative basis, today's $10 plugs are cheap in comparison, and the $15 models have really only kept pace with inflation.

What are they?

As already explained in brief, plugs and minnows are lures with a 'body' made of timber, plastic, resin or some other material (rarely metal). They may be hollow or solid, and come in a vast array of sizes and shapes. Most carry from one to three sets of hooks. These are usually trebles, but may be doubles or, in very rare instances, single hooks. Some have built-in rattles (usually lead shot or tiny ball bearings), others don't—although it's worth remembering that almost all body baits make underwater noises by virtue of the fact that the hooks and rings rattle and tap against the lure. This is especially noticeable on hollow bodied plugs, where the body itself acts as a kind of resonator or amplifier.

One major feature separates the plugs and minnows into two broad classes or sub-groups. That feature is the presence or otherwise of a diving plane, variously known as a 'lip' or 'bib'.

Let's take a closer look at some of the major members of the body bait clan, starting with the most popular and diverse of all-the floating divers.

Floating divers

As the name implies, these float on the surface at rest, but dive down through the water column when retrieved. They achieve this act of magic by virtue of

Big trout show a marked preference for big minnows—in this case a 13 cm Rapala.

Jointed lures

Almost all of the lure styles covered in this section are available in jointed or articulated versions. These joined lures have never been especially popular with Australian anglers, possibly due to suspicions concerning the strength and durability of the connection. It's also a fact of life that jointed lures are a little more expensive than their rigid, one-piece stable-mates.

The benefits of jointed lures mainly centre on their action characteristics. Put simply, jointed lures have a stronger swimming action, and are capable of obtaining that action at a lower retrieve speed. This makes them ideal for night and dirty water use, where dead slow presentations are often the ticket.

Jointed floating minnows such as the jointed Rapala Originals are particularly effective night time offerings for trout. They will swim at a dead crawl and appear to be highly attractive to nocturnal browns and rainbows.

Try to carry at least one or two jointed patterns among your collection of plugs and minnows, and use them when conditions are tough.

Casting sinking minnows in rivers is a very effective tactic and works in all seasons.

a plastic or metal lip affixed under their nose—the diving bib.

How deep these lures run, and how rapidly they attain that running depth, is dictated by the size and angle of the bib, as well as a combination of more subtle design characteristics, which act upon their hydrodynamic performance.

At one extreme, we have the ultra-shallow runners like the Manns Minus One and some of the Bombers and Bagleys. These run anywhere from 15 centimetres to 45 centimetres beneath the surface on a standard retrieve.

In stark contrast are the super deep divers, characterised by plugs such as Whopper Stopper's Hellbender, the biggest Hot 'N' Tot, Manns Plus 30 and Aussie products like John Ellis' StumpJumper or Rob Smith's Boomerang. All these lures are capable of achieving running depths in excess of five metres on a standard retrieve, and will dig even deeper when trolled.

Even more importantly in most fishing scenarios, they have steep diving angles and achieve their running depth rapidly.

You can make a pretty fair guess at the running depth and dive angle of a floating minnow by looking at the design of the bib. If the bib is large in relation to the lure's body size, and protrudes almost dead ahead (in line with the axis of the body), the lure will dive deep and fast. Exactly how deep and how fast depends on things like balance, buoyancy and precise bib shape, but at least you know you're looking at a deep runner.

On the other hand, a relatively small bib, which protrudes down from the minnow's body (at a sharp angle to its axis) will run at a very shallow operating depth. Again, precisely how shallow will depend on buoyancy, body shape and what you do with the rod and reel (more of that soon).

Action in diving plugs is also quite variable. It is a product of two things: the battle between the lure's inherent buoyancy and the diving forces exerted by the bib and the flow of water over the lure's body.

On the one hand, we have the fairly strong, side-to-side beat or wobble of the American-style, fat-bodied plugs. At the opposite extreme is the much tighter 'shimmy' or partial roll of the European-style, thin-bodied minnows. In between are many combinations and nuances.

As a rule of thumb, the strongly swaying 'wobblers' are more appealing to outback natives (cod and goldens, particularly) and Australian bass. The shimmying minnows work better on trout, salmon and surprisingly, barramundi. It's hard to say why this should be so, but most experienced anglers would agree. Of course, there are many exceptions, and the next big brown trout to fall to a 'bass plug' certainly won't be the first!

Buoyancy is a fascinating variable in diving lures. Very buoyant models tend to have good, strong actions and work at a range of speeds. However, when paused they bob quickly towards the surface, which can be a drawback in certain situations, but very useful when it comes to floating the lure over a snag or weed bed.

Sinking divers

Most sinking divers look very much like floating divers. However, as the title implies, they do not float on the surface at rest. Instead, they sink through the water column at varying rates.

Surprisingly, few of the really deep running deep divers are sinking lures. I say surprisingly, because it would seem an advantage in attaining depth to have a lure with negative buoyancy. In practice, this generally is not the case, though there are exceptions, such as Bagley's Dredge.

Instead, most sinking divers are mid-depth running lures. A typical example is the very popular and productive CountDown (CD) range from Rapala. Comparing a Countdown and Floating Original Rapala of the same length (say, a five or seven centimetre version) tells us a lot about the differences between these two minnow styles. First, the sinking model will be significantly heavier and will, as a result, cast much better than the floating model. This can be a distinct advantage in many situations, especially when casting from the shore of a lake or large river.

Second, the sinking model will run slightly deeper than the floating version, even if the retrieve commences immediately the lure lands. This can be exaggerated by waiting for the lure to sink a little ('counting it down') or using a relatively slow retrieve with the rod tip at or below the surface. Again, this may be advantageous.

Finally, the sinking version of the lure will have a less pronounced action and a narrower band of speed tolerances—usually weighted towards the faster end of the scale. In other words, you need a bit of pace to get most sinking minnows working. This is especially noticeable with plugs like to Rapala Mini Fat Rap and the new CD-3.

This need for greater speed, and the less clearly defined action of sinking lures, is something of a drawback, and is the price we pay for the improving the casting and depth-covering capabilities of the CountDown style.

Working sinking divers

Most of the tips given for floaters can be applied to sinkers, though obviously you can't let them rest on the surface after splashing-down. Similarly, there is little point in cranking a sinker down. Instead, you should let it sink of its own negative buoyancy. As can be imagined, this is extremely useful for working the face of an underwater ledge or cliff, or for getting a lure to a good depth right alongside a tree before commencing the retrieve. This is where sinking minnows and plugs really shine, and allow you to do things no floater is capable of.

Because sinkers have less inbuilt action and narrower speed tolerances, it is especially important that they be fished on thin line and with loop knot connections. You simply can't afford to dampen their action any more than necessary.

Remember, too, that you can't 'float' a sinking diver over a snag, or let it drift quietly on the surface while you unpick a backlash or eat a sandwich. These may be important considerations in shallow or very snaggy water.

Such drawbacks are well worth living with when you consider how a sinking diver can be cast in the face of a stiff breeze, or allowed to drop right against the base of a drowned tree before being pulsed away in a little cloud of mud guaranteed to drive redfin or yellowbelly bonkers!

Rattle baits and sonics

This group of body baits consists of bibless hollow and solid lures with a vaguely fish-like, flat-sided

Optimum lure selection - plugs, minnows and topwaters			
Scenario	Best lures, type/examples	Best colours C: Clear Water D: Dirty Water	Best presentation, retrieve/speed/action.
Trout/Stream	Euro' Minnows/Rapala Originals and CDS, small Nilsmaster, Killalure Trout Bait, Rebels, etc. Bass Plugs/McGrath, Bill Norman, Bagleys, Halco Combat.	C: Silver, gold, black, green D: Fluoro green, yellow, hot pink.	Brisk, steady and with occasional rod sweeps. Slower at night or in dirty water.
Trout/Lake	As above with emphasis on sinking minnows and slightly larger patterns. Some use of prop baits and topwater lures at night.	As above with emphasis on matching forage species.	As above, plus counting and cranking down.

shape and an eyelet on the upper, front surface. Most contain rattle chambers, and are characterised by the likes of the Cotton Cordell Rattlin' Spot, Manns' Leroy Brown, Rapala Rattl'n Rap, Bill Lewis Rat-L-Trap and Bagley's Rattle Shad. A few older style 'sonics' are completely solid and don't have rattles. They were claimed, instead, to produce sound waves through their body shape and action. Most appear to have been displaced by the rattling noisemakers.

All of these lures sink, though the rates vary. Most carry a pair of treble hooks. Held in mid-water on a tight line, they will ride roughly level, not tilting down appreciably at head or tail.

Sizes and weights vary considerably among rattling lures, though there are few true mini-baits in this category. For general freshwater fishing in southern states, the 5–8 cm versions are best.

Regardless of their size, most sonics have a tight vibrating action of the retrieve or lift, and a flashing flutter on the drop. Because the hooks are exposed and there's no bib to 'trip' them over snags, they hang up easily in timber and rocks.

Working rattle baits

Rattle baits are at their worst on a straight, cast-and-crank retrieve. For this reason, they're also pretty ordinary troll lures—unless the rod is hand-held and worked fairly actively.

Rattle baits are meant to be worked stop-start, lift-drop and up-and-down. They particularly shine when jigged vertically on pinpointed concentrations of bait or fish.

This is not to say that rattlers can't be effectively cast and retrieved. They can, and often with outstanding results. The trick is to use frequent pauses, bursts of speed and/or pumps and lifts of the rod.

Just like a sinking diver, a rattler can be cast tight to cover and counted down right alongside it. Unlike a sinking floater, a rattler is working actively all the way down—shivering and rattling in a most appealing way.

Rattlers should be worked on slightly heavier tackle than most other lures. This is because strikes often come very close to cover and on partially slack line, giving the fish a good head start. In addition, frequent hang-ups in submerged timber demand a

Many anglers prefer a darker coloured monofilament for lurecasting in both rivers and lakes.

line capable of withstanding some abrasion. And of course, it goes without saying that you'll need a Tackleback or some other de-snagging device!

Stickbaits

Stick baits are the simplest of all surface or top-water lures. To make a stick bait yourself, simply take a long, thin-bodied floating minnow and snap the bib off! Indeed, you don't even need to do that with some minnows. The Bomber Long-A, Rapala Husky and Rapala original 11 and 13 all make great stick baits with their bibs intact.

As you might have guessed from that description, a stickbait is a long, thin floating lure with a little inbuilt action. As such, it is one of the harder artificials to work, as almost all the action comes from the angler. However, the effort can be worthwhile, as a thoughtfully fished stickbait can prove the undoing of some big, cunning fish at times!

The most famous of all stickbaits is the Heddon Zara Spook and its smaller stable mates, the Zara Puppy and Zara Pooch. These very plain, cigar-shaped lures with their chin-mounted towing points actually spawned a presentation and retrieve style of their very own, known as 'walking the dog'.

Walking the dog involved constant rod work and/or a stop-start retrieve that causes the lure to bob and weave in a most enticing manner, rather like a small mammal, lizard or snake swimming across the surface. It can be used with all stick baits, and is deadly on saratoga, surface feeding barra and big bass. This strategy also has definite applications for night feeding brown trout, but as far as I know, this is an avenue yet to be explored in Australian waters.

The other major retrieve style for stick baits is called 'ripping' or 'jerk baiting', and is mostly used with the long, thin, shallow-running minnows such as the Bomber Long-A, Rapala Husky, and 9, 11 and 13 centimetre Rapala Originals. It involves using quite violent rips and stabs of the rod that cause the lure to dive half a metre or so, then bob quickly back to the surface.

Prop baits

A prop bait is basically a stickbait with one or more metal or plastic 'propellers' added at the nose or tail. Australian fishing writer Rod Harrison coined the name 'fizzers' for these lures, and it is extremely apt, accurately describing the way in which they fizz and fuss across the surface.

Good fizzers have been traditionally hard to come by in Australia, with supplies never exceeding a dribble, and local anglers slow to wake up to their incredible fish catching potential. Some of the best American-made prop baits are: Smithwick's Devil's

River mouths are great places to fish lures.

Horse, Strike King's Prop Scout, Heddon's Dying Flutter, the classic Heddon Tiny Torpedo, Cotton Cordell's Crazy Shad, Woodwalker's Woodchoppen and the Highback Spin-N Shiner. About the only one of these available on a reasonably regular basis here is the Tiny Torpedo, which is a killer on Australian bass, not to mention sooty grunter and jungle perch in northern waters. It has also taken more than the odd trout.

Which brings us to a unique and unusual prop bait. The Heddon Fish Cake, Wigston's Devil Cake, has carved itself a niche on the Aussie scene almost entirely by virtue of the effect it had on Lake Pedder's giant browns back in the 1970s and early '80s.

Cast from the windswept points of that big Tasmanian lake on black, moonless nights, and crawled back towards shore with agonising slowness, the Fish Cake produced some mind-boggling captures. These included lots of browns in the five kilo class, and at least a sprinkling of fish to almost double that weight! The rinky-dink little hooks on the Fish Cake, and the way in which giant browns often fumbled and miss-hit the things, also guaranteed that there'd be plenty of 'one that got away' stories during those halcyon years at Pedder.

Fish Cakes faded from the limelight with the

general demise of the Pedder phenomenon, but it would be wrong to think that they stopped producing fish. I know some great browns taken at night in Victoria's Lake Toolondo and NSW's Eucumbene and Jindabyne on these bizarre plugs. Surely they have potential elsewhere, too?

The trick with all prop baits and fizzers is to work them just fast enough to get the props thrashing, and to incorporate plenty of pauses in the retrieve. Most strikes come just as the lure is 'fizzed' after a sweaty-palmed pause of several agonising seconds. Thrilling fishing, and definitely not for the faint-hearted.

Crawlers

The so-called crawlers are yet another family of surface plugs, best represented by the Heddon Crazy Crawler and Arbogast Jitterbug. These are both hollow bodied plastic lures (though the originals were made of wood) fitted with metal attachments designed to create action and surface activity. In the case of the Crazy Crawler, these consist of a pair of hinged metal 'arms' that do a pretty fair imitation of the butterfly stroke as the lure is retrieved. On the Jitterbug, a concave metal 'scoop' acts as both a popping face and a kind of hydrofoil that causes the lure to sit up high on the water and skate when retrieve with any significant speed.

Although these two timeless classics are usually spoken of in the same breath, they are actually quite different in their actions and best presentations. The Crazy Crawler requires a reasonably sustained and relatively quick (by surface lure standards) retrieve to really work. On the other hand, the Jitterbug is a more versatile plug that may be fished with a variety of retrieve strategies from the slowest stop-start to the quickest skating dash.

Because of these differences, the lures are best employed in separate situation. The Crawler is ideal for covering lots of water where fish could be just about anywhere, while the Jitterbug is better suited to painstaking, pin-point work around known fish-holding structure. Interestingly, though, the 'Bug can also be used as an open water ground cover, whilst the same role reversal doesn't really work with the Crazy.

Both lures work on trout, especially after-dark browns.

Miscellaneous

There are several lure types that appear to fall outside the major headings just discussed, but which still fit loosely into the body baits classification, and which are simply too important to pass over. Most obvious of these are the Flatfish and their clones, and other diving, non-bibbed plugs such as Tiny Tads,

Tadpollies, Canadian Wigglers, Lazy Ikes and Hot Shots.

The Flatfish are so important, and different enough in their design and use, that they deserve separate treatment. However, it's worth mentioning in passing that none of them make particularly good casting lures. This is mostly due to their unusual hook set-ups and their light, wind-resistant bodies.

Tiny Tads, Lazy Ikes and Hot shots are another kettle of fish altogether, and represent an extremely useful class of artificial for the lure caster.

These plastic bodied, slow sinking bibless lures originated for a style of American fishing that has become known as 'hot-shotting'. It involves a wading or boat-borne angler paying out line down a relatively swift river current or set of rapids, then holding his lure against the flow to give it action. The lure is worked through likely pocket and lies, then paid back further to work new water. At the same time, the angler may change his position in the current to allow the lure to reach un-fished areas. Think of it as a kind of 'stationary trolling' if you like!

Hot shotting is extremely effective on spawn run salmonids, most noticeably steelhead (migratory rainbows) and chinook salmon. However, it also works on resident stream trout and some other species, such as the American walleye.

I believe the most obvious local applications of hot-shotting are for trout and salmon in reasonably large, strong flowing rivers like Victoria's Goulburn or the upper Murray and Murrumbidgee in NSW and the ACT. I feel it would also be an extremely workable technique on New Zealand's South Island chinooks in rivers like the Rakaia. I'd be surprised if no-one's tried it.

Putting it all together

Armed with the information in this section, you should now be able to make some intelligent decisions about the plugs, minnows and surface lures applicable to your favoured styles of fishing, and start to assemble a workable kit of hardware.

As explained, these lures aren't cheap. Putting a dozen of them in your tackle box will most likely set you back in excess of $100. For that reason, you owe it to yourself to choose the best, most applicable options and optimise your chances.

Think about the options, choose carefully and lean towards patterns with multiple applications. That way, it's possible to put together a dozen plugs and minnows that will adequately cover your usual needs, and which should also have something to offer on those odd occasions when you come across something completely new and different. *Steve Starling*

Spoons & Wobblers

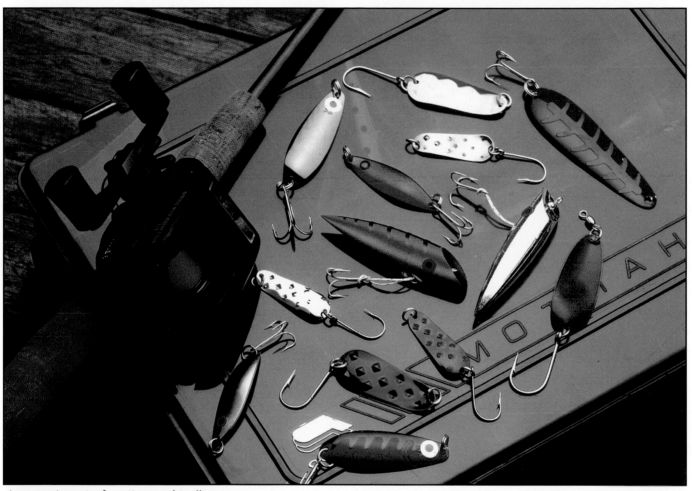

An assortment of casting and trolling spoons.

According to legend, the fishing spoon was invented by a careless servant in feudal Europe. While shaking the crumbs from his master's table cloth, he accidentally dropped a silver teaspoon into the river that flowed alongside the manor. As the item of cutlery twinkled towards the bed of the stream, a huge old pike shot out of the weeds and engulfed it!

The story doesn't tell us if the servant was eventually fired (or worse!) for sawing up his employer's cutlery to make lures. However, there's little doubt that this is exactly how most of the early spoons were manufactured.

Down through the ages since their accidental discovery, spoons have become an absolutely basic lure style for freshwater angling around the world. In more recent years, they have also made a limited impact on the saltwater scene, although it is still the freshwater lure fisherman who keeps the spoon makers in business.

Today, spoons are available in an incredible array of shapes, sizes, materials and finishes. In this section, we will be looking solely at casting spoons, and leaving aside the so-called 'flutter spoons' which are really only applicable to the trolling scene.

Casting spoons

Modern casting spoons fall into five main categories (see table). The first three categories—Colorado, Indiana and needle—are all standard, metal spoons, differentiated solely by the shape of their bodies. The fourth type—the Tassie lures—are an Australian design made of clear plastic and lead, while the fifth and final class—weedless casting spoons—are American bass lures not often encountered in this country.

Beyond these five groupings, spoons vary considerably in their precise design, weight, thickness and action. As a general rule, however, they retain the 'teaspoon bowl' concept of being convex on one side and concave on the other. It is this 'bowl' shape that creates the lure's action as it is drawn through the water.

Most spoons have quite specific speed tolerances: they simply do not work below or above a certain speed band. In some models, this band is very narrow. Whenever you use a spoon, you should spend some time experimenting with retrieve rates in order to establish to ideal speed brand of the model in use. To help you with this, remember the following rule of thumb: long, thin spoons made of thick gauge metal require more speed, while short, fat spoons made of thin gauge metal require less speed.

Colorado spoons

These spoons are wide bodied-almost round in some cases. They offer maximum water resistance and have a wide, rolling or 'thumping' action, which is best at low retrieve speeds. At higher speeds they will spin (causing line twist), or plane to the surface and begin jumping.

Because of their design, Colorado spoons do not cast as well as some other styles. This is due to their inherent air resistance and their tendency to 'float'

or 'kite', especially in a head-wind.

These criticisms aside, 'Collards' nonetheless offer superb low speed actions and plenty of flash and vibration. They are great in dirty water or low light conditions, and also excel when cast upstream and retrieved just a little faster than the current. Light gauge 'Collards' can even be dead drifted with the current on a reasonable tight line, bouncing and trundling over the stream bed in a most attractive manner.

Indiana spoons

These are slightly more elongated and a little narrower than the fat bodied Colorado spoons. 'Indians' represent the largest spoon group of all, as characterised by the evergreen Wonder Wobbler, and the Evil Eyes and Daredevils.

Indiana spoons handle more speed than Colorados and have a greater retrieve rate tolerance band, although this is dictated to a large extent by the thickness or gauge of the metal used.

Optimum Indiana action involves a partial roll and strong tail kick or flutter. They definitely should not spin. Any spoon that spins is being retrieved too rapidly.

Casting a wobbler in this deep tannin stained pool will often bring the big trout up from the bottom.

Spoon Lore

Spoon	Description	Action	Popular examples	Applications
Colorado	Wide bodied, almost round.	Strong wobble at low speed, good flutter on the drop.	Wonder Imp, Kilty Pike Spoon, Halco Wiggler, K.O.Wobbler, Red Eye Wiggler, etc.	Small streams, dead drift or slow downstream retrieve, jigging and 'jiggling'
Indiana	Intermediate between Colorado and needle.	Good wobble and tail wag at medium speeds. Lighter gauges have stronger actions.	Wonder Wobbler, Gibbs Ko Ho, Big Bugga Spirt Spoon, Halco Marvel Wobbler, Les Davis Hot Rod, Pegron Cocktail.	Streams, rivers and some lake casting. Extremely versatile and variable in design.
Needle	Relatively long, thin body. Only heavier gauges are applicable to general casting	Tight wobble or sway with a partial roll at medium to quick retrieves.	Abu Toby, Pegron Minnows, Gibbs Candlefish, Wonder Crocodile Spoon, Wonder Spoon, etc.	Ideal for shore casting in lakes and larger rivers. Some smaller, lighter gauge models are useful in streams and creeks.
Tassie	Lead body insert with clear plastic case and 'wings'. Coloured foil wrap around insert.	Strong side-to-side wobble and partial roll at moderate to fast retrieves.	Tassie Devil, little Devil, Wigstons, Cobra, Tillens etc.	Designed for trolling, but very popular with shore based casters working lakes and dams. Some application in big rivers.

Needle spoons

These are the long, relatively thin spoons made famous over the years by classics such as the ABU Toby, Gibbs Candlefish and our own Pegron Tiger and Mountain minnows.

Needle spoons require a little more speed than the two previously described styles. They also cast better, especially in heavier metal gauges. This combination of characteristics makes needle spoons extremely popular with shore-based anglers working lakes and impoundments. With a good needle spoon, it is possible to cover more water in less time and still fish it effectively.

Conversely, needle spoons have less application in small streams, although some of the smaller, lighter gauge models work well, even on tiny trout creeks.

Tassie lures

These specialised lures evolved out of the Tasmanian trout lake scene, and although primarily intended for trolling, they have found great favour with shore-based and boat-equipped lure casters.

The basic construction style of the Tassie patterns involves a lead or alloy insert encased in a clear plastic body with plastic 'wings' or 'fins'. The overall result is a heavy, yet strongly-actioned lure with the visual impression of being quite small.

The most famous representatives of this breed are the Wigstons Tassie Devils, Cobras and Tillens. All have pronounced side-to-side wobble and partial roll, and when swimming properly, cause the rod tip to pulse rhythmically. Optimum speed bands are usually quite brisk, especially when compared to

Colorado and Indiana spoons. They are more in line with the operating speeds of medium to heavy gauge needle spoons.

Tassie lures cast like bullets, making them ideal for covering big bodies of water. Their rather heavy splash-down and rapid sink rates render them next to useless in small streams, though some anglers use them to good effect on larger rivers.

Castability versus action

In all spoon selection for lure casting, there is a certain trade-off between castability, sink rate and action. Heavy gauge spoons (those made of thicker metal) cast extremely well and sink rapidly, but have less pronounced actions and require a higher retrieve speed. Light gauge spoons do not cast as well, but have stronger actions and demand less speed.

All of this means that heavier gauge spoons, especially needles and Tassie patterns, are best used for covering large areas of water at a reasonably rapid rate—as when walking the banks of a lake, dam or big river. Lighter gauge spoons in Colorado and Indiana configurations are better for smaller streams, creeks and little rivers. Exceptions occur, of course, but these guidelines are certainly useful when it comes to assembling a selection of spoons for your favoured angling styles and most frequently fished waters.

A word on size

Unfortunately, many US spoons, and quite a few from Europe, are too big for local conditions. This is because they have evolved to match larger forage (prey) types such as the alewife, herring and smelt common in waters like the American Great Lakes, and also because they are used on big sea-run salmonids, pike and muskellunge, as well as smaller, land-locked trout and salmon. Be aware of this when shopping for spoons!

The ideal size range for Aussie trout and salmon is between four and seven centimetres (about 1 ½ to 3 inches), not including hooks. Opt for the lower end of this range in rivers and the higher end in lakes and you won't go too far wrong.

To fish a spoon

Once the correct speed band for a particular spoon has been established, most lure casters simply shift into the mechanical cast-and-crank routine. This catches fish (particularly lake-dwelling rainbows and Atlantic salmon), but it is a long way short of optimum usage.

This first refinement all spoon casters should try is the 'count down' technique. This involves counting off the seconds as a spoon sinks until you feel it touch bottom (indicated by a sudden slackening of the line). This count can then be used as a benchmark to thoroughly explore the water column.

For example, it takes a certain spoon twelve seconds to reach the lake bed in a specific location. A count of ten seconds will have it running a metre or so clear of the bottom at the start of the retrieve. A five second count will see it swimming in mid-water.

Mix up your counts. Try one cast at eleven seconds, the next at two and so on. This is often more productive than methodically working down or up through the water column in one second increments. The reason for this is that a surface or near-surface swimming trout could easily swim into and out of your casting zone without you ever knowing it while you painstakingly count the lure down twelve, eleven, ten seconds and so on.

Next, try pauses mid-way through a retrieve. Most spoons (especially Colorado and Indiana styles) flutter attractively on the 'drop', attracting strikes and frequently turning followers into takers. To facilitate solid hookups, make sure that your spoon drops on a reasonably tight line, and be especially alert for hits just as you recommence the retrieve after a pause.

Light spoons in clear fast running rivers are an excellent choice.

These variations are particularly effective on brown trout, golden perch, small cod and redfin-fish that you might never know were there if you stick purely to the cast-and-crank routine.

Colours and finishes

This subject could occupy an entire article on its own, though I believe that it may be a little less important than many anglers think. Suffice it to say that the old theory of dull or naturalised colours in clear water and brighter, fluorescent hues in dirty water still has much merit. Similarly, copper, brass and gold metal finishes (especially 'hammered' patterns) are better performers in stained or murky water, while silver and nickel may have the edge in clear conditions. At night, try black.

Most spoons are coloured on one side with paint, enamel or reflective tape, and have a bare metal finish on the other side. Some anglers like to experiment with the addition of colour or prism tape to the 'blank' side of the lure. It is arguable if this significantly improves results. Instead, I prefer to simply keep my lures clean and bright by washing them occasionally and if necessary,

polishing the exposed metal with Brasso, silver polish or even toothpaste. However, be sure to thoroughly rinse the lures afterwards in running fresh water, as some of these chemicals may leave odour traces unattractive to sensitive fish.

A final word

Finally, it should be stressed that spoons work, and along with spinning blade lures (spinners), should form the core of any lure collection used primarily for trout or salmon.

Spoons may not be as trendy or sophisticated as some of the latest and greatest bibbed minnows, plugs or jigs, but they probably catch a greater tonnage of salmonids in Australian waters each year than all of these other hardware styles combined! Don't be afraid to carry a good, basic selection of spoons and spinners in your lure casting tackle box, and tie one on whenever in doubt.

That careless servant who dropped the teaspoon in the river back in the Middle Ages could hardly have guessed what he'd started—a lure fishing 'revolution' that changed the face of freshwater angling forever! *Steve Starling*

Lurecasting wobblers along lake shores early morning and in the evening can produce results.

Winged Wonders

If you asked most Australian trout anglers if they ever used spoons for their fishing most would likely reply that they seldom ever use this type of lure. In reality the Tasmanian 'Cobra' is really a type of spoon, albeit a heavy, uniquely-shaped one.

Every size, shape and description of spoon has been manufactured over the years, but nothing else comes close to these little plastic and lead marvels. The Cobra style of lure has an amazing scope to accommodate a broad range of applications for almost any fishing condition. With the addition of a couple of new innovations to this style of lure Australia's most popular and successful fresh water fishing lure has become even better!

The Cobra design has been around for a very long time now, with a range of manufacturers producing it. Most offer a range of colours and finishes, but remarkably most of the differences are little more than cosmetic. Slightly different weights or subtle changes in the body size or wings have been the norm. However, two manufacturers, Lofty's Lures and Wigstons Lures have now introduced a new deeper diving lure. Although both have no doubt been researching this problem for some time it's very interesting to note that their approach and the finished products are very different. Because of this the two lures, Loftys Wide Wing Cobra and Wigstons Dual Depth Tasmanian Devil, each have a unique action and a range of applications. No matter what your personal preference in brand may be, both styles deserve a place in your tackle box to accommodate a range of conditions.

The main purpose of this section is to help create a better understanding of how this lure works and what you can do to improve your success and catch rate.

There are over a dozen manufacturers of winged tassies or cobras in Australia now.

There are a number of factors that play a part in how well your lure is presented to a fish including your choice of line, rigging, hooks, boat speed and the lure itself.

Lines

One of the most critical factors in achieving optimum performance from any lure is line selection. The line you choose for a particular application deserves a lot of careful consideration, after all it's your main connection to a fish. Though the importance of line selection has been emphasised countless times, a lot of anglers seem to pay little attention to this detail when it comes time to spool up for a fishing trip. The age-old adage about getting what you pay for certainly rings true when it comes to line selection.

The technology and choice available to anglers in the form of monofilaments, co-polymers, braided gelspun, and fluorocarbon lines is really quite staggering. The array of manufacturers and brands of lines, along with the price and availability, seems to have expanded enormously in the past ten years. The most important areas for consideration with trolling applications should be line diameter, stretch and abrasion resistance.

When you are trying to decide on a line for trolling, keep in mind that lines which are primarily made for casting are not the answer for trolling. In many of our impoundments you will encounter submerged trees, rocks, fences etc, that will really test out your line. Trolling lines need to be fairly tough with good abrasion resistance and low stretch, not soft and limp like a good casting line. The brand you choose is a personal preference, but buy as good a quality line as you can.

Generally line diameter for downrigging is not as crucial as when surface trolling. Having said this you still need to choose your line carefully. Your selection of line for downrigging should take into consideration what type of line release clip you use and the type of downrigging you intend to do. If you are constantly chasing the bottom in snag ridden waters you need to consider a tougher abrasion resistant line. For most Australian conditions line from 0.20 to 0.30 mm will handle just about any fishing situations.

Line diameter plays a major role in how deep your lure runs when trolled or retrieved. Thinner diameter lines allow your lure to run deeper and optimize the lure's built-in action. In most applications diameters in the 0.18 to 0.22 mm range are your best bet for trolling Cobra style lures on surface or flat lines. My personal choice for flatlining is line of 0.20 mm diameter. Lines of this size (and of course all others) can vary enormously in breaking strain from one

Single Hooks Versus Treble Hooks

Single hook rigs are becoming more popular with anglers who troll winged lures for salmonids in Australia. They have several advantages over the traditional treble hook that most anglers use. The major advantage is their resistance to weed collection. In shallow lakes that are filled with ribbon or strap weed, there is often a lot of broken strands that constantly foul on the treble hook rig. With a single hook, the incidence of fouling is reduced markedly and means that you spend more time productively fishing. As a bonus a single hook provides a better hook up ratio because there is only one hook trying to penetrate the hard mouth. This means that all the pressure applied with the strike drag goes directly to the one hook point and is not spread over three hook points as is the case when using a treble hook. Also during the fight as the fish shakes its head, the pressure between the hook points on the treble may be great enough for one or two hook points to be removed. With a single there is no opposing force to remove the hook so they hold onto fish far better than does a treble hook.

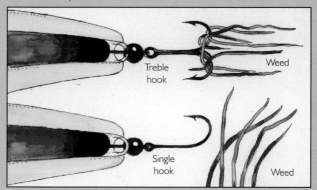

White Tassie Devils have been real fish producers under certain conditions.

Rigging a Wide Wing Cobra

Rigging a Wide Wing Cobra entails running the line through the centre of the body starting from the end that is widest. The line is then run through the supplied bead and tied off to a treble hook. Alternatively, you can also tie the line off to a treble hook rigged on a split ring. Rigging in this manner allows the Wide Wing Cobra to reach depths of 3.2 metres, although this will vary with trolling speed and line diameter.

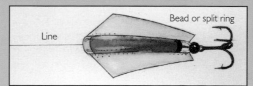

maker to another. Most major brands are between 2–4 kilograms breaking strain for 0.20 mm line which is more than adequate for most trout trolling applications in our impoundments.

Today's new generation of gel spun braided lines are amazing to use. Surface trolling or flat lining with braided lines is almost like learning to troll again. The amount of stretch in this type of line is so minimal as to be almost non-existent. Your first hook-up on a fish will amaze you with what you can feel: every head shake or flap of a fish's tail is transmitted through this type of line. If you have never used this type of line keep in mind that with so little stretch you need to run a very light drag and use a rod that is soft enough to be forgiving and act like a shock absorber. Lines such as Fireline, Spiderwire and the Australian-made Platypus are all excellent performers.

Line stretch and resultant breakage can be a problem with some lines. Stretch is usually difficult to detect until you snag up or try to land a big fish. Ordinarily you can see or feel the difference when your line has stretched and not fully recovered. When your line is stretched it may also show up as a different colour, most noticeable with darker coloured lines. To avoid problems like this most line manufacturers recommend that you cut approximately 1.5–2.0 metres off your line and retie your lure after landing a big fish or getting snagged. It's probably something that most anglers don't do often enough.

Rigging a Dual Depth Tasmanian Devil

Rigging the Dual Depth Tasmanian Devil in the standard mode entails running the line through the centre of the body, then through a bead and finally tying it onto the hook. This can be varied by passing the line through the body, then tying it directly to a split ring which has a hook attached to it. This allows the lure's action to be far more pronounced. Rigged in this method the Dual Depth Tasmanian Devil runs at 2.5 metres in depth.

Rigging in the deep running mode, the line is passed through the moulded hole in the nose of the lure, through the body, through the bead and then it is tied to the hook, or you can use the split ring method. Rigged in the deep running mode, the Dual Depth Tasmanian Devil reaches a depth of 3.6 metres. It must be noted that these depths can vary with line diameter and boat speed.

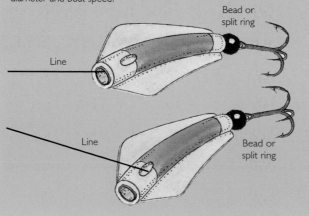

Line

Bead or split ring

Line

Bead or split ring

Rigging Tricks

One tried and true approach to rigging this style of lure usually entails passing the line through the body of the lure, through a small plastic bead, and tying it to your choice of hook. As the lure moves through the water the hook is pulled up tight against the bead which in turn locks it in one position. To gain the most from your lure the hook should be able to move freely. Using a split ring instead of a bead, allows free movement of the hook.

Hook Options

The standard hook that comes with most of these types of lures is usually a single treble hook. After experimenting with several different types of hooks for the last three or four years, I almost never use a treble behind a Cobra style lure. Invariably, if you have my sort of luck, when you hook up on a small fish they seem to have a real knack for getting caught with all three prongs of a treble in their mouth.

When you try to get the treble out you can do a lot of damage to the fish. Because catch-and-release is something I firmly believe in and want to practise, I now use single hooks. My favourite pattern is an open eye Siwash hook. An Eagle Claw 210NA, VMC 9171N1 or Gamakatsu saltwater fly Siwash hook are all brands I've used with great success.

One of my main concerns when changing over to single hooks was whether or not the hook-up rate would be as good as with a treble. My experience has been that it's even better and rarely do you seem to fail to hook a fish. The Siwash pattern of hook is used extensively in the US and Canada for salmon and steelhead. This type of hook features a very long point, short shank, wide gape and usually has an open eye which you can crimp over a split ring. Regardless of what brand or pattern of hook you choose, make sure you keep it razor sharp.

Deep Innovations

The introduction of the new Wide Wing Cobra and the Dual Depth Tassie Devil should prove to be a real bonus for trout anglers in the coming seasons. Wigstons Dual Depth Tassie Devil uses a combination of dual towing points and heavier weight (20 grams) to achieve a deeper diving lure. On the other hand Loftys Wide Wing Cobra adopts a wider wing and retains the 13 gram weight of the standard Cobra. My experience with these lures has shown that they are both fairly sensitive to speed. The Dual Depth needs a slightly faster (2.5–3.5 km/h) because of its heavier weight while the Wide Wing seems to operate best at slower (1.5–2.5 km/h) speeds. Both lures need to run at the right speed to avoid line twist. As with any lure of this style watching the rod tip can tell you what's going on with the lure. If you pick up weed on the lure it will change the action of the rod tip alerting you to the fact that it's time to bring the lure in to clear it. Both of these lures work equally well for lead lines, flat lines or downrigging, but my preference is to run them on a flat line or surface line. For downrigging I prefer to run a standard lure of 13 grams or the smaller 7 gram model when conditions warrant.

Most anglers seem to shy away from the 7 gram or 25 gram size lures for trolling but I've found they are both very productive. The size of the forage fish you are trying to imitate should dictate what size your lure should be. The 25 gram lures have a very strong action that can be extremely productive if you are chasing big trout and salmon. The smaller 7 gram size lure is great for shallow water or weed bed trolling and has the same great action. The 7 gram is also an excellent choice of lure when you want to run a slider off the downrigger.

With the advent of the new deeper diving lures, the amazing range of colours and sizes means Australian anglers have a greater choice than ever before. Dollar for dollar these lures are some of the best value tackle around, so no matter which brand you choose you can support a unique Australian product! *Bill Presslor*

Rigging for Shallow Running

Trolling in waters that contain weed beds extending almost to the surface can call for a different approach to lure presentation. If the forage fish your attempting to imitate are very small the 7 gram size Cobra or Tasmanian Devil may be the answer. If your offering needs to be larger, but still run shallow, consider trying a technique shown to me by a good friend a few years ago. With a standard 13 gram lure take a sharp knife and pare the clear plastic wings of the lure. What you want to end up with is a wing that is 3-4 mm wide at the head of the lure tapering to about 1-2 mm at the tail. Altering the lure this way will allow it to swim much shallower (approx 0.4 m), but still retain the same action and great for targeting shallow weed beds.

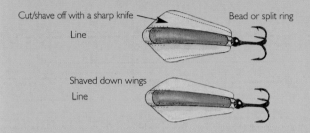

A last option if you do not want to alter your lures is to turn them around so that the tail end points towards the rod tip. Rigged in a similar fashion (line through centre of lure, through bead and tied off to the hook), a tighter action is achieved and the trolling speed can be increased without the lure blowing out. The reduced action and higher speed of trolling reduce the running depth of the lure by half and can be an easy way to troll above weed beds.

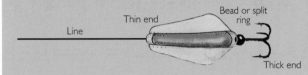

Trolling winged lures is one of the most consistent ways to catch trout in lakes.

The Mechanics of Trolling

Catching fish trolling is just as demanding and skilful as lure-casting. Bait-fishing and even fly fishing. To regularly catch fish anglers must be willing to work hard and set up their boats correctly to do the job.

The variables in trolling are just as complex as any other form of fishing-boat and lure/bait speed, lure depth and dropback, choice of lure (colour, shape, surface or diver) or bait, use of attractors (dodgers, cowbells), water temperature and light, use of downriggers or not-the variables go on and on. Then there's the decision of where and when to fish.

Trying to make sense of all this can confuse so many anglers that they give up in frustration and simply refuse to consider these options at all.

Resist the temptation! Read on and I will go through some concepts that have been successful for me and for a number of top trollers who I have observed over the years.

Boat mechanics and troll speed

Without a boat you can't troll, and without a motor you're going to get very fit rowing. Your boat and motor are the most important trolling tools so look after them!

The amazing advancements in the last ten years have been in the running of the bigger outboards. Almost all medium outboards of 20–40 hp now offer smooth trolling performance which, in some cases, rivals that of even the smaller motors.

The improvements of greatest interest have been in the 50–100 hp motor range. These are now engineered to run in gear, at idle, without fuss.

Expect and demand a lot from your modern outboard. The key seems to be the technician who tunes the motor prior to delivery, as the manufacturers are all producing beautiful machinery these days.

Once on the water there are a few technical an practical points to keep in mind. The first is that you should never equate a given throttle setting (or corresponding rpm on the tachometer) to a set speed. Wind, can slow down or speed up a boat considerably when trolling. You may be able to monitor your speed off your depth sounder (if you have that facility), but remember that even these are very inaccurate below 2 kilometres per hour. The best bet is still to troll those standard lures short and observe their actions.

Towing buckets is still a viable option to slow down. Here these anglers are downrigger trolling in Creel Bay, Jindabyne in May for bottom hugging pre spawn brown trout.

Trolling the Drop-offs

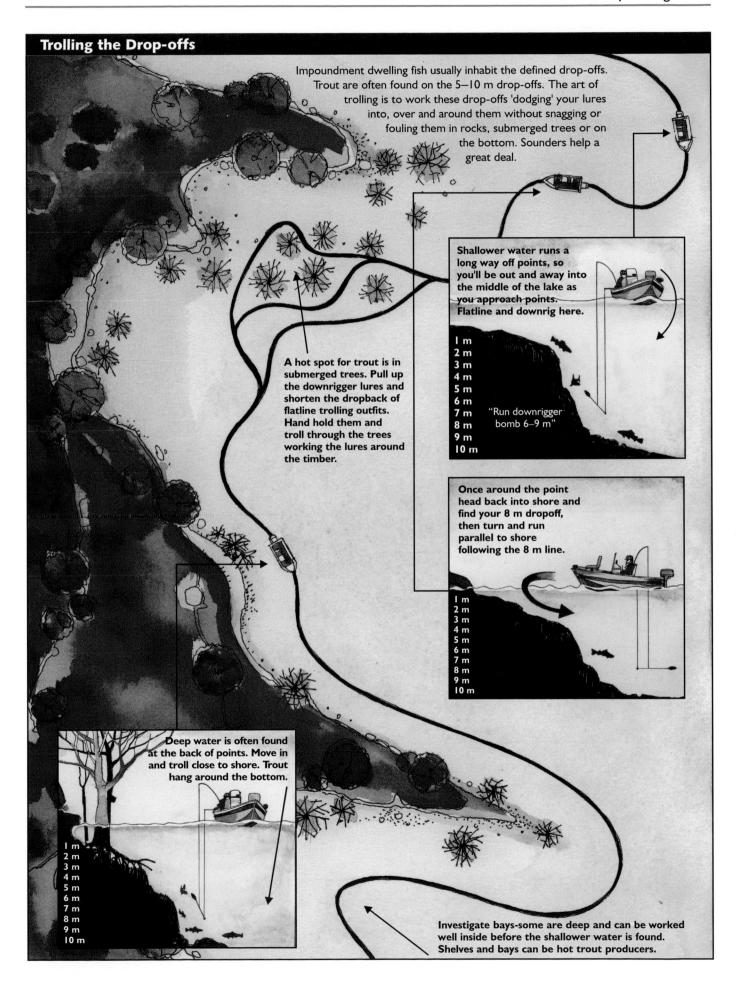

Impoundment dwelling fish usually inhabit the defined drop-offs. Trout are often found on the 5–10 m drop-offs. The art of trolling is to work these drop-offs 'dodging' your lures into, over and around them without snagging or fouling them in rocks, submerged trees or on the bottom. Sounders help a great deal.

Shallower water runs a long way off points, so you'll be out and away into the middle of the lake as you approach points. Flatline and downrig here.

1 m
2 m
3 m
4 m
5 m
6 m
7 m
8 m
9 m
10 m

"Run downrigger bomb 6–9 m"

A hot spot for trout is in submerged trees. Pull up the downrigger lures and shorten the dropback of flatline trolling outfits. Hand hold them and troll through the trees working the lures around the timber.

Once around the point head back into shore and find your 8 m dropoff, then turn and run parallel to shore following the 8 m line.

1 m
2 m
3 m
4 m
5 m
6 m
7 m
8 m
9 m
10 m

Deep water is often found at the back of points. Move in and troll close to shore. Trout hang around the bottom.

1 m
2 m
3 m
4 m
5 m
6 m
7 m
8 m
9 m
10 m

Investigate bays-some are deep and can be worked well inside before the shallower water is found. Shelves and bays can be hot trout producers.

Propeller pitch and gearbox ratios

Boat speed and rpm will also vary greatly from motor to motor, brand to brand and horsepower size to horsepower size.

Propeller pitch can make a big difference in the top speed of your rig, assuming the motor has enough power to hold the revs. At trolling speeds however, the propeller pitch will make less of a difference and it is your gearbox ratio that will determine what your lowest speed will be.

Trolling plates are the ideal solution to slowing big rigs down to trout trolling speed. This one is a beauty as the Trol-A-Matic is automatic.

A big bag of browns and a rainbow taken on a downrigger and specifically targeted with a depth sounder.

Another important factor that determines lower end trolling speed is the lowest idling speed of your motor. Good mechanics can achieve minimum idle speeds of 500 rpm in gear, but if you can get something in the range of 600–700 rpm smooth and falter-free then you're on the right track.

Slowing down

Trolling anchors

Nowadays with the move to bigger boats and motors, the final choice of a trolling motor is less complex. Years ago the small auxiliary was the choice for reliable trolling as the bigger motors had an inherent desire to oil up. Nowadays that is not the case, so a good option is to troll with the main motor. If tuned correctly it can easily idle in gear all day! Modern fishing ignition systems and oil injection have ensured that. The main difficulty now is to find a good service mechanic to do the tune.

Now a system is required to overcome the 'faster' lowest troll speed of these bigger units. Baffle plates are popular in the United States but have been unavailable here. They are also expensive and although they reduce trolling speeds on big outboards, they also reduce steering sensitivity, which causes problems in wind and tight situations.

The modern day answer is to pull a trolling anchor off a 1 m tow rope from the bow of the boat. A trolling anchor is very similar to a sea anchor and the advantage of rigging it from the bow is that it effectively slows the boat-in most cases it will halve the slowest trolling speed. It also improves the steering at trolling speeds.

Trolling anchors are essential for all freshwater trolling rigs where speeds need to be slower and controlled better, and where anglers don't want to use auxiliary trolling motors.

Trolling auxiliaries

Many anglers now just prefer to troll with the main motor whether it is a 20 hp or an 80 hp with a trolling anchor.

There are alternatives though, and these range from small hp auxiliaries, which can either be hand steered at the transom, or connected to the main motor and directed through the steering system.

Then there are electric outboards that can be transom or bow mounted. These are ideal for slow trolling and are the alternative trolling option on my boats. They are perfect for slow trolling baits. They are also the ideal method of propulsion when 'stall trolling' amongst trees.

Lure speed

The choice of lure speed (troll speed) is just as important as the choice of lure colour. On some days it is often the most important factor.

Each lure has a range of speeds which will work. Sometimes they will elicit hits at their lower end speed range and sometimes at their upper end speed range. In addition some lures are built to be used in a high speed range (eg RMG Scorpion, Bennet Merlin or Tassie lure) while others will only work in a 'slow' speed range (eg Flatfish, Kwikfish or Magnum Dodger chain). For a full detailed guide to lures and their preferred speeds refer to Frank Prokop's *Lure Encyclopaedia.*

Your lure speed is generally (discounting currents) determined by the boat's trolling speed. Knowing just how fast your boat's trolling speed is for any particular rpm is the first key to effective trolling. Once you know how fast your boat moves through the rpm trolling range—usually 500–1200 rpm—you can select lures which best fit those ranges.

I use a simple and practical way to determine what will or won't work at various rpm ranges. I select a few test lures and troll each one separately and very short (only some 3 m off the rod tip) through a range of speeds. I hold the rod in my hand so I can easily see whether the lures are working correctly or not and note the range through which each works best.

I also test the lure while the boat is moving into the wind as well as when running with the wind. Remember that waves, and even currents (yes, there can be currents in big impoundments!), will have an effect on boat speed and thus the lure speed. A boat running downwind at a set rpm will result in a quicker troll speed than that running into the wind at the same rpm.

A Tassie Devil lure is great for an upper speed range verification. This lure is a great trout taker at high speeds with its formidable sway. When it breaks the sway and starts a full circle loop you're right up at the

Trolling Anchors - Slowing big and small boats

Towing buckets behind the boat is ineffective as they are in the lee of the hull and have minimum drag. The key is to troll a proper trolling anchor from the bow of the boat of the winch eye. This will slow the biggest boat and motor combination to acceptable trolling speeds. It can also slow many conventional 8–40 hp motors to mudeye trolling speeds. To prevent accidentally taking off with your trolling anchor in the water, hook the trip string over the throttle lever.

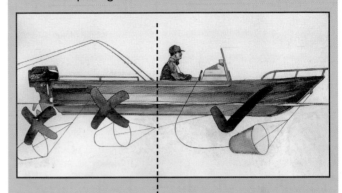

Don't tow the trolling anchor or let it sit near or behind the centre of the hull because it will cause steering problems.

The correct position is one quarter the way down the hull from the bow. This position allows for full drag and enhances steering, even in strong winds.

top end speed rating for most lures. CD Rapalas and some metal lures will also work around these speeds but generally not a lot of lures regularly operate at this speed.

For the lower range verification I try an X4 Flatfish. If the boat can throttle down slowly enough to pull one of these without looping it, then you're right down in low gear range—a speed perfect for trolling baits such as mudeyes behind Ford Fenders or dodger chains.

Sometimes trout just love lures trolled this slowly, especially brown trout, yet at other times they are attracted to a lure working at speeds many freshwater anglers would find amazing. Often rainbow trout roaming the middle of lakes and feeding on daphnia prefer lures trolled at these higher speeds. If you're trolling baits for trout (either worms or mudeyes behind attractors such as cowbells or attractor chains) then you must throttle right back-slow is the go! Top speed for these baits is around normal Flatfish trolling speed, so work down from there.

Trolling spoons are lures with a very specific action. They are meant to flutter. Almost every trolling spoon made has some sort of bend or set which makes it dart when swimming and flutter when sinking. All spoons have a speed at which swimming action is optimised. Too fast and they spin out of control, too slow and they are drawn through the water like limp spaghetti. A properly worked flutter spoon will imitate a baitfish not only in size and shape but also in action. Changes in speed and direction are all that are required to initiate a good flutter spoon action. The vertical flutter down and tumbling action, the 'rise' and then a 'normal' troll speed for a couple of minutes puts the life-like bait fish action into your spoons. For the downrigger troller especially, understanding the basics of flutter spoons will increase success no end. The boat driver can initiate the action by varying trolling speed and employing manoeuvres such as stalls, turns and even circles.

Speed tuning lures

A critical aspect of trolling is to know your lures are working correctly at a given trolling speed. One way to speed-tune lures is to monitor their action through the rod. Hold your rod and let the lure swim back 2–3 metres. Observe the action and learn to recognise the feel of this action through the rod. Try a few speed variations and watch the lure's changed action and match that with the feel through the rod tip. Then let the lure out to its desired dropback and again feel its action through the rod. Train yourself to know what is the best speed for a particular lure or set of lures and learn how to monitor its action through the rod and by observing the movement of the rod tip. Learn how to match lures to speed too-if you want to try the slow approach then use lures designed to be worked slowly and which have plenty of action at slow speed. If you're prospecting new water and moving fast then clip on lures which will work at that speed.

Trolling Hints

1 Trolling is not just restricted to lures—baits, both live and dead can be rigged to troll at all speeds.
2 If you start catching fish in an area stay there.
3 Scents do work when applied to lures and they can make the difference at times. I can only surmise that they mask unpleasant odours and pheromones.
4 If you're not catching anything and there is trout about try decreasing your trolling speed to slow the action of the lure and make it dive. Hand-hold the rod and jig it to give the lure an extra burst of speed and action.
5 Troll right in and around submerged and exposed trees. Shorten dropback, hold your rod and 'work' the lure around the trees as you troll.
6 When flatlining, the quickest way to get your lure up off a shallowing bottom or snag is to stand up and hold your rod above your head-this will raise your rod quickly.
7 Never troll in a straight line. Turning into and away from drop-offs gets the lures close in. Turning also speeds outside running lures and stalls inside running lures. This attracts strikes.

Too many trollers worry too much about the speed they are doing and forget that the important key is to have a set of lures, which are working correctly at their current trolling speed. No lure action equals no fish. Likewise, too much speed will spin a lure out of control. The obsession amongst Australian anglers for slow trolling speeds works against many who use the majority of lures-many require more speed for action. Slow speeds are useful but only with lures which work at that pace.

Trolling rods

Trolling for trout requires a rod neither so inflexible that it masks the lure action, nor so sensitive that it just bends over under the lure's pull. It also pays to have variety in the length of your trout trolling rods as it is helpful when trolling four flatline lures on the surface. The longer rods (2.5–2.6 m) should be used on amidships rod holders at 90° with their lures well back behind the boat. The shorter rods are placed in the stern rod holders horizontal to the water but at 60° to the boat, with their lures running in shorter and deeper.

Finding fish

Finding fish in a lake is a challenge for everyone as they seem to turn up in the most unexpected places-or do they?

The vertical approach to finding fish, using diving and sinking lures through to downrigging is well detailed elsewhere in this publication, but just where to apply these techniques makes all the difference between success or failure. To just downrig and flatline troll over deep water out in the middle of a reservoir will produce, at best, rainbow trout and rat browns.

Instead, working the drop-offs in impoundments is what you should be really be doing as this is where fish usually hang out! This involves trolling into the shore (and hence into and along the drop-off shelf) at about 45° to the shelf with downriggers down and flatlines out. Monitor the water depth on the sounder and turn back out into the safety of the deeper water when the downrigger bomb approaches the shelf bottom.

By repeating this you will work your lures well and put them where the big rainbows and trophy browns live. This method can be used in Eucumbene, Eildon, Dartmouth , Wyangala or any trout lake in the country, wherever there is clear, safe, deep water alongside structure.

Other vertical considerations include temperature, visibility, clarity and oxygen content. A temperature gauge or probe can be a big help here in finding those preferred zones.

Coriolis Force Currents

Surface current will concentrate food along this shore!

Subsurface current could make this shore a hot spot!

Surface currents are deflected 10–25 deg left of the wind direction due to Coriolis effect.

Wind Direction

Wind Direction

Surface current

Rebound current

We all know the earth spins on its axis with gravity keeping us from being thrown off. In fact at the surface of the earth at the equator the spin speed is 1,667 km/hr and this has a direct effect on water currents caused by winds. In the southern hemisphere it deflects to the left of the wind direction and in the northern hemisphere to the right, with the greatest effect being evident the further one gets from the equator.

Maximum deflection is around 45 degrees and is only observed in oceans but a deflection of 10 to 25 degrees is normal in freshwater lakes.

Finding fish—laterally

Just how do we chose which shore of a lake or reservoir to concentrate our efforts? One great place to start is to fish where fish food accumulates. Fish food may be forage (little fish), aquatic insects, drowned terrestrial insects, daphnia (water fleas) or shrimps and snails.

Steady winds on a reservoir will establish a subsurface current which will move towards the windward shore. These currents will collect and move poorswimming food such as drowned terrestrials, plankton, daphnia and the like which, in turn, will attract baitfish or forage. Eventually the larger fish will be attracted by the collection of food.

Remember though, the Coriolis force will affect the direction of that current, pushing it to the left of the wind direction in the Southern Hemisphere. This phenomenon is a result of the earth's rotation. The deflection is greater the larger the body of water and the further one moves away from the equator. Typically the deflection is around 20° or so. It also affects rebound currents.

Applying this knowledge indicates it is best to troll down and across wind with it blowing on the starboard (right) side of the boat. This sets your lures trolling straight down the current. But you will need to speed to stop your surface lures hanging in the current.

If a downrigger is towing lures at around 8 m then you're in the opposing rebound current and they may start to spin out of control. I have observed trolling speed differences of up to 2 km/hr between the surface speed and the bomb speed. When in doubt, it is best to follow the currents to the left of the wind direction and never just troll in a straight line.

Remember too that pelagic fish, such as trout and salmon, will nearly always face the current so best presentations are usually down-current.

Likewise structure oriented fish will concentrate where underwater currents bring them food, so look to shores well to the left of the wind direction for places to fish.

In the end

The bottom line is that fish are where you find them and they'll turn up in what you'll often think is the strangest of places, but just as often we can work out where the fish are, get the right lure, correct trolling speed and enjoy success. One of the golden rules of fishing is to thoroughly search an area for all possibilities and never leave an area which is producing fish for another area that you think might produce fish! You may never find the first one again! *Bill Classon*

Depth Sounders

Depth sounders are now part of the normal gear found on fresh water boats trolling for trout. There couldn't be a serious trout troller who doesn't use one.

How many anglers want to know how to get the best out of their depth sounder, but find it difficult to accurately interpret its read-outs? When fishing on a well-known Victorian lake, I once had a Fisheries officer challenge my sounder read-out. He believed the many fish arches were just invented by manufacturers to please the angler. 'Give me a net any day and I'll tell you if they're trout or not,' was his attitude.

Later in the day when the sounder was still on the same settings and we travelled over the same terrain the fish arches failed to appear! Did the machine forget to place the arches or had the trout moved to another part of the lake? I know the latter was the case but I was hard pressed to enlighten the officer.

Depth sounders do read fish, as well as bottom structure, bait and mid water objects. Combine a bit of experience, a dollop of observation and some intelligence and an angler can roughly estimate the size of the fish sounded. If he also knows what fish species live in the water he may have an educated guess at the species of fish appearing on his read-outs. Remember professional fishermen are earning a living by using depth sounders in salt water, and to a lesser extent in the fresh water.

The fish finder
A fish finder is basically made up of three parts, a main processing unit with display, a transducer and a power supply.

Power supply
The power supply is usually a 12 volt battery. The unit is best connected to the starting battery, not to the trolling motor battery, as the trolling motor will cause electrical interference to the sounder. Better still have a separate battery to eliminate any possibility of electrical interference.

Transducer
The transducer is the unit that emits sound waves and receives signals. It is made from a 'plastic/resin' material that absorbs electrical energy and emits sound energy. These sound waves travel at 1.5 km/s in water. When they hit a 'target', i.e. bottom or weed, rock, fish or even dramatically different water temperature layers, part or all of the sound wave is bounced back. The transducer is also super sensitive to returning sound waves and converts them back to electrical energy.

The main unit
The main processing unit amplifies this electrical energy from returning sound waves and feeds it to the display unit where it may burn a mark, via a stylus, on heat-sensitive paper (X16 Lowrance) or activate a pixel in a liquid crystal display (X70 Lowrance or Humminbird Wide).

Remember that a fish finder has to do two things: it has to send a signal down and then has to listen for return signals from targets.

The main unit determines the number of electrical pulses per second sent to the transducer, which then emits them as sound waves. If the electrical pulse was continuous there would be no time for the transducer to receive signals back from the sound waves it produces. The length of the electrical pulse is measured in microseconds (μs), and can vary from 30–2000 microseconds. Between each pulse the transducer 'listens'.

Power and sensitivity

These are two entirely different things.

The power of a unit is fixed and cannot be altered. The unit's power is indicated by the strength of the electrical pulse it sends to the transducer and consequently determines the strength of the sound waves it emits. Generally more powerful units will perform better than less powerful units but that is certainly not the only determining factor on the performance of a sounder.

The power of a unit can be measured in two ways; either Peak to Peak or root mean squared (RMS). Basically both systems measure the same thing. Scales of measurement are different but outcomes are equivalent. Simply remember RMS is equivalent to one eighth of Peak to Peak value. For example 600 watts Peak to Peak is the same as a unit with 75 watts RMS power. The higher end recreational power units are of the order of 800 watts Peak to Peak or 100 watts RMS.

The sensitivity or gain of a unit is an entirely different thing to its power. It is the ability of the main processing unit to listen for signals returning to the transducer. This listening must be done in the time between power pulses being sent out. The operator can adjust the sensitivity on the unit and it works by increasing the sensitivity of the transducer to signals bouncing back off the objects below.

Sensitivity should always be set at the highest level possible without flooding the display with unwanted information. To get the best reading from your

Fish Arches

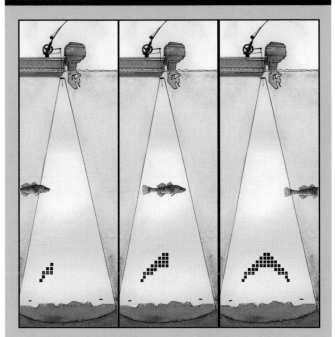

A perfect fish arch depends on the unit having enough vertical pixels to register the distance between the first contact with the fish (the furthest away and the lower edge of the arch) and the 'middle' contact under the boat, the closest and the top of the arch. As the fish passes through the other side of the sounding cone (again a long contact point to the fish) the other lower edge of the arch is marked. The fish must also pass straight through the cone.

Sounder Technology and Fish Arches

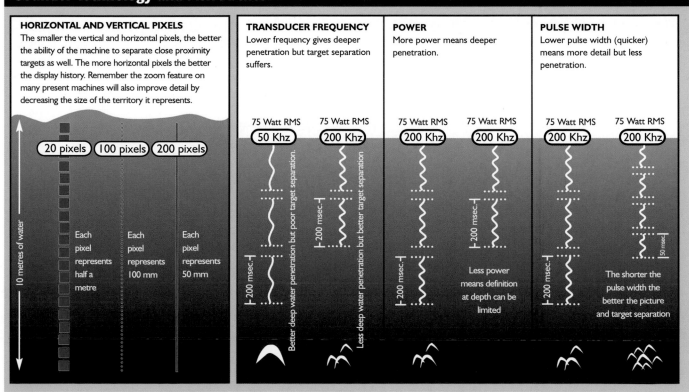

HORIZONTAL AND VERTICAL PIXELS
The smaller the vertical and horizontal pixels, the better the ability of the machine to separate close proximity targets as well. The more horizontal pixels the better the display history. Remember the zoom feature on many present machines will also improve detail by decreasing the size of the territory it represents.

20 pixels · 100 pixels · 200 pixels

10 metres of water

Each pixel represents half a metre

Each pixel represents 100 mm

Each pixel represents 50 mm

TRANSDUCER FREQUENCY
Lower frequency gives deeper penetration but target separation suffers.

75 Watt RMS — 50 Khz
75 Watt RMS — 200 Khz

200 msec.

Better deep water penetration but poor target separation.

200 msec.

Less deep water penetration but better target separation

POWER
More power means deeper penetration.

75 Watt RMS — 200 Khz
75 Watt RMS — 200 Khz

200 msec.

200 msec.

Less power means definition at depth can be limited

PULSE WIDTH
Lower pulse width (quicker) means more detail but less penetration.

75 Watt RMS — 200 Khz
75 Watt RMS — 200 Khz

200 msec.

50 msec

The shorter the pulse width the better the picture and target separation

Tranducer Selection

50 kHz wide cone angle transducer
- Best for deep water in salt water (80–500 metres)
- Good for deep reef and canyons.

200 kHz narrow cone angle transducer
- Best for deep fresh water (30–100 metres)
- Will pinpoint bottom features and fish.

200 kHz wide cone angle transducer
- Good choice for shallow fresh water (5–50 metres)
- Will cover a good spread of bottom and fish.

Multi component transducer (5–100 metres)
- Usually called wide or broadbeam.
- Good choice as provides best of both worlds.
- Targets fish under boat and to the sides.
- Good deep penetration and shallow water spread.
- Many existing sounder models will accept a wide beam-check with manufacturer.

sensitivity control, first turn it to full. You will notice small marks and dots will appear all over the screen. This is unwanted 'static' and means the unit is 'listening' too carefully. Slowly reduce the level of sensitivity until the clutter marks just disappear. This allows for full sensitivity or 'listening' for returning signals. Normally sensitivity or gain should be run at ¾ to full. In deeper water, 15–20 m, you'll find full sensitivity is usually required. Remember gain is not power! Power gets it down there and sensitivity picks up the returning sound wave.

Computer power

What determines the quality of the readout displayed on the screen is the Central Processing Unit (CPU). This processing unit interprets the returning signals to the sounder and how well it does this is determined by each manufacturer's specifications.

Lowrance for instance has developed excellent interpretive software for its sounders and has been long regarded as the industry leader with this technology. Its

software, called ASP or Auto Signal Processing, helps display fish as fish, and weed as weed. Similarly, the other main player in the Australian market, Humminbird, has been developing the processing power of its sounders to enhance their displays.

Transducer frequency

What transducer frequency is best for you?

In freshwater I use a 200 kHz transducer with a 20 degree cone angle. This gives me excellent detail and a good balance of bottom coverage.

A higher frequency transducer produces shorter wavelength soundwaves; a lower frequency transducer produces longer wavelength soundwaves. The shorter the wavelength (higher the frequency), the better target separation and the better detail on the screen.

However short wavelengths have poor depth penetration per power unit pushing them. So a short wavelength sounding from a 200 kHz transducer will give an excellent display of detail in shallow water (up to 30 m) but will require plenty of power in the unit to hold detail beyond that (at least 50 watts RMS, and better at 75 watts).

A 50 kHz transducer is best for really deep water (in excess of 80 m), as the longer wavelength requires less power to penetrate deeper. Remember though that the display will not be as good, as target separation and detail is reduced.

An analogy is that a 500 kHz transducer pumping 50 watts RMS gives a performance that would require 1000 watts RMS with a 400 kHz transducer! Most freshwater units run at 200 kHz as that frequency gives good target separation and detail to around 50 m with a power of around 75 watt RMS. Rarely, if ever, would one see a transducer of 400 kHz or higher, as it requires a lot of power to push it and also suffers from interference from other electrical units.

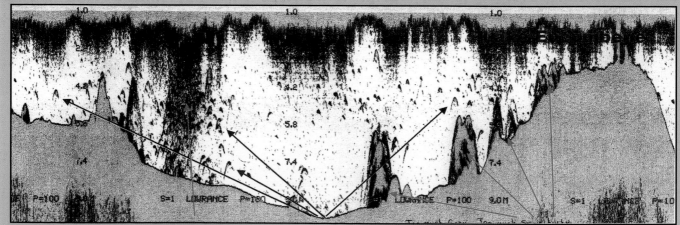

Sounding Sample - Sensitivity - Grey Line - Trout - Submerged Trees

Too much grey line   Too much sensitivity   Trout   Submerged trees

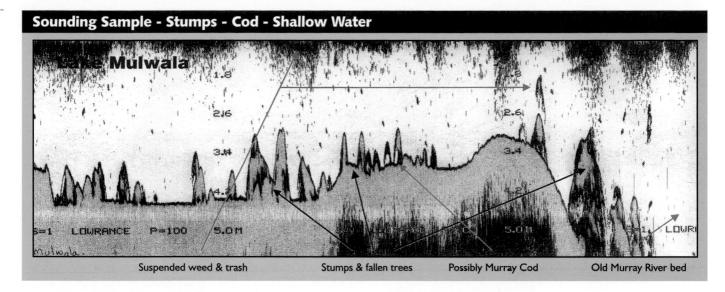

Sounding Sample - Stumps - Cod - Shallow Water

| Suspended weed & trash | Stumps & fallen trees | Possibly Murray Cod | Old Murray River bed |

Do sounders scare fish?

No evidence exists either in US or here that indicates sounders scare fish. The pulse from a transducer is heard as a click.

Transducer cone angles

Yet another factor in effective sounding is the cone angle of the transducer. 'Wider means better' is not necessarily the case, though in general, the wider the cone angle the more area is covered at each depth.

To get a handle on things, a 45 degree cone angle will sound an area of bottom of 8.3 m diameter, a 20 degree cone angle will cover an area 3.5 m in diameter and an 8 degree cone angle covers 1.4 m diameter.

So one may say the best scenario is to go for a 45 degree cone angle transducer to get maximum coverage.

Maybe so, but there are limitations with transducer design that prevent a 200 kHz transducer from having a cone angle much over 20 degrees. Similarly, transducers that operate on a 50 kHz frequency usually are restricted to a cone angle of 45 degrees or more! Don't be tempted to use a 50 kHz 45 degree unit to get wider, better coverage in shallow water–it won't work. Remember the longer wavelength sound wave from a 50 kHz will give very poor target separation and a poor 'picture' in shallow water when compared to a reading from a 200 kHz transducer. Use a 200 kHz, 20 degree transducer, which is my personal choice, or go to the new multi-component, 'wide' or 'broadbeam' type transducers that pulse at 200 kilohertz.

'Wide Views'

'Wide views' have become popular in recent years and basically come in two forms—3D and broad view. Both are generated from a multi-component transducer consisting of three, four or six crystals, usually with a 20 degree angle all overlapping to give a wide, 45–90 degree coverage.

A broad beam, or broad view, type transducer displays screens like a standard display. The better units will actually tell you whether the fish is to the left or right or under the boat, as with the X55A Lowrance.

With the Hummingbird Wide View and Wide Vision a dual beam transducer is employed. The transducer fires two beams of sound, one at 16 degrees and 200 kHz and the other at 53 degrees and 455 kilohertz. The screen picture is a result of information from both with solid fish symbols indicating fish under the boat and hollow symbols being fish at either side.

In the case of the 3D sounders their screen picture is generated from multi-element transducers, usually 16 degree elements. These all overlap and give bottom coverage of around 45–53 degrees. The three dimensional screen image then plots the boat and shows where the fish are with respect to the boat.

There is a place for 3D and wide pictures, but they certainly aren't the only and best option.

Target separation and better 'pictures' in depths 0–40 metres

There are a number of variables that at their optimum and when combined, produce good target separation and hence great 'pictures', but the most important two are frequency/wavelength and pulse width.

As the wavelength of the sound emitted from the transducer increases, the frequency of the sounding wave decreases and as does the target separation.

The wavelength and frequency is fixed and determined by the transducer. Hence the 50 kHz transducer won't separate targets as well as a 200 kHz transducer.

The second factor is pulse width. As explained earlier a sounder operates by firing a pulse of sound repetitively from the transducer rather than a continuous uninterrupted sound wave. If it transmitted continuously it would never have any time to listen or receive signals!

The pulse width is the measurement in time that the sound wave is emitted. Short pulse widths (30–100 μs) provide maximum target separation and at 30 μs, according to Lowrance specifications they can separate fish as close as 50 mm! At the other end of the scale, a pulse width of 1000 μs has a target separation of about 1.5 metres.

If you need to penetrate into deeper waters a longer pulse width is required to enable more energy to be imparted into the sound wave. Sounders nowadays automatically adjust pulse width as the 'Set Lower Limit' is increased. A few years ago some sounders allowed the operator to manually adjust the pulse width. All the soundings displayed in this section were made using a Lowrance X16 paper sounder for ease of reproduction. The X16 is one of the few sounders that allowed manual adjustment of pulse width.

HINT: Always set the lower limit on your sounder to a figure that will account for the current depth of water under the boat. I.e. if you're in 9 m of water don't set the lower depth at 30 metres! This will cause the programming in the sounder to increase the pulse length and reduce target separation. Set the lower limit to 10 m and reap the benefit of better target separation due to a lower pulse width.

Remember too that high power units will give better readings because with high power they can hold the lower pulse widths in deeper water. Hence a 30 watt RMS unit may have to be programmed to

200 μs pulse length in 20 m of water but the 75 watt unit may be able to hold onto a 100 μs pulse as it has more power to shoot that short pulse down. By being able to hold a shorter pulse width the target separation and readout is improved.

Auto mode

My advice is don't use it! Always switch to manual. This will allow you to set the gain or sensitivity to maximum and will allow the optimum lower level to be set to maximise screen view.

Fish ID

Likewise I don't like to use the fish symbol ID features on recreational sonars. Turn them off and concentrate on learning to read true signals on your sounder. With fish ID I've often seen the top of a downed tree shown as a school of fish! Take the time to look and learn and aim to work out the local water first. You're likely to know what to expect and hence can relate the 'picture' on the sounder with the fish and structure under the boat. Nothing beats experience! Remember turn up the gain to get best soundings.

Grayline

Most sounders now incorporate Grayline and its purpose is to help interpret bottom type and structure as well as enhance separation of fish. Grayline is a lightening of the lower portion of all sounding features, from the bottom to the fish themselves!

I use Grayline to distinguish what sort of bottom I am over. Set the gain or sensitivity first then add Grayline, but only a little. Unlike gain/sensitivity, which gives best results between 75–100 per cent of maximum, the Grayline should only be set at 5–15 per cent. Only add Grayline until it first shows up on

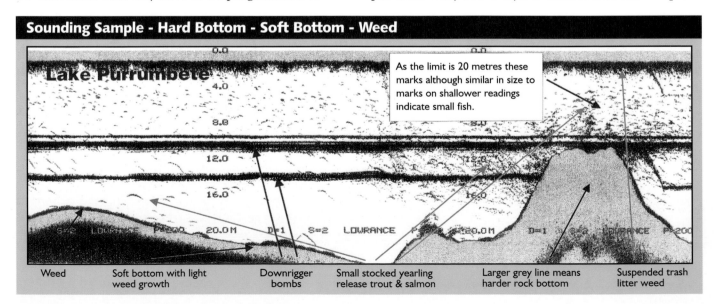

Sounding Sample - Hard Bottom - Soft Bottom - Weed

As the limit is 20 metres these marks although similar in size to marks on shallower readings indicate small fish.

| Weed | Soft bottom with light weed growth | Downrigger bombs | Small stocked yearling release trout & salmon | Larger grey line means harder rock bottom | Suspended trash litter weed |

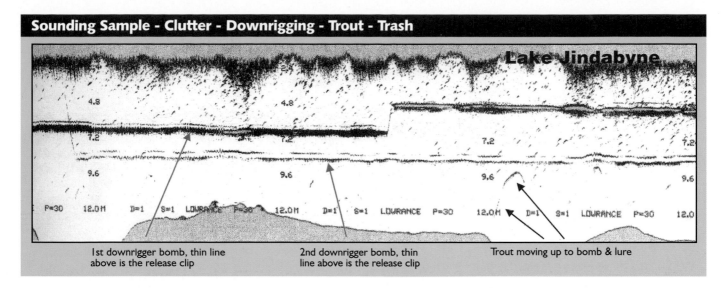

Sounding Sample - Clutter - Downrigging - Trout - Trash

Lake Jindabyne

1st downrigger bomb, thin line above is the release clip

2nd downrigger bomb, thin line above is the release clip

Trout moving up to bomb & lure

the bottom sounding. Have a look at the examples and you'll get the idea.

As for bottom interpretation, a wide band of Grayline means a HARD bottom-rock, stone etc. A SOFT bottom will narrow or even make the Grayline disappear! If you've got structure like rocks, timber or weed off the bottom you can also interpret it with Grayline. With the Grayline set correctly, a rock pile or timber will have plenty of Grayline underneath but weeds, being soft, will remain black underneath.

LCD and pixels

All major recreational sounders now use an LCD screen and an array of pixels to display information. Many of the soundings shown in this article are from a paper sounder-the X16 Lowrance-which, in my opinion, is still the best and most sensitive sounder ever made. However, sounders like the Lowrance X70 and the Humminbird Wide Vision produce very detailed 'pictures' with their 200 vertical pixel screens.

We talked about target separation before and spoke about achieving a target separation of 50 millimetres. A continuous tone paper sounding only enhances this, but a coarse pixel screen blows it out the back door!

For example an LCD screen with only 50 vertical pixels means that in 20 m of water each pixel can represent nothing better than 400 millimetres. So your electronics might be great, but the coarse pixels on the LCD screen will defeat the detail!

New units with 200 vertical pixels will allow a detail of 100 mm separation in 20 m of water and in 10 m of water this would equate to 50 mm separation.

Fish arches

The ultimate sounding is marking fish as solid arches.

Easier said than done, many say! The theory of the perfect fish arch is that the sounding cone must pass over the fish evenly and the fish must pass through the centre of the sounding cone.

It must also be recognised that many sounders still mark fishes as just that, a mark! The interpretive software incorporated in each sounder goes a long way here and manufacturers are very guarded about protecting their software. Lowrance has an excellent reputation for 'arching' fish and distinguishing features. Humminbird, in my opinion, still had a way to go some years ago but today is producing a product that must be taken seriously.

Suppression

Suppression filters out return signals not sourced from the transducer in the first place. Mostly this involves electrical noise from the engine and increasing suppression can aid soundings made at high speed. Set suppression to zero, otherwise information can be lost as it will affect your return signal too!

Interference

This is another system to filter out unwanted noise, usually associated with other sounders operating in the same area. Obviously the use of the interference control will affect your sounding quality and I aim always to use zero interference.

Summary

The purpose of this discussion is not to recommend a particular sounder but to give you the knowledge to get more from your existing sounder and to make a better, more informed discussion when next purchasing a unit. Balance your budget with your requirements, and remember sounders never lie, we just interpret them incorrectly! *Bill Classon*

Downriggers

By now most anglers should know what a downrigger is and how they work. But for many anglers there are still unanswered questions and unexplained techniques to explore.

Trolling is one of the most effective methods of taking our inland fish, but to take full advantage of it you need to determine where the fish are located in the water, both in the horizontal and vertical planes, and get your bait or lures there.

When fish cannot be reached by baits trolled on the surface, or with surface and deep diving lures, many anglers use either leadcore line, wire line, paravanes or sinkers to get them down deep. These devices have one common drawback in that the weight needed to get the required depth can spoil the fun of fighting a fish. Even worse, increasing the trolling speed or bait/lure depth means that you'll have to increase the

weight or size of the devices and the problem is then compounded.

The best method to attain a given depth is to use a downrigger. In its simplest form, this is just a weight attached to a spool of wire line, and a release clip attached to either or both of them. The clip holds the fishing line (with lure attached) at a certain depth until a fish strikes. It then releases the fishing line from the weight and wire line, allowing you to fight the fish freely.

There are a lot of other reasons why downrigger fishing is better than the others mentioned above. Repeatedly setting a lure at the same depth is easy with the downrigger. If your downrigger has a counter, you just note its reading at the depth you want, and return it back to that reading the next time. If there is no automatic counter, just count the

The art of downrigging was foreign to most Australian anglers before 1990, now there'd be only a few serious trollers who don't use one.

number of revolutions of the spool handle or, even simpler, just read the track on your depth sounder. All other methods are hit-and-miss and imprecise, particularly when a distance of only a couple of metres can mean the difference between a strike, and your lure or bait being ignored.

With downriggers you can spread a number of lures out over the vertical plane and have a better chance of locating the fish. If a pattern begins to emerge that fish are holding at certain depths, you can concentrate exactly on these hot spots. Vertical hot spots can coincide with thermoclines, temperature breaks, visibility, clarity changes and levels of dissolved oxygen.

Another advantage of using downriggers is that you can avoid problems with floating debris and weeds, especially during autumn. When trolling surface lures the debris or weed catches on your line and then slides down the line to foul the lure.

By downrigging just under the rubbish you can avoid the problem and catch more fish.

Mounting the downrigger

Most downriggers I see on boats have been mounted in inappropriate positions, usually across the stern on tiller-steered craft. Positioned there, the downriggers are difficult and inconvenient to use as you must continually turn around to work them. The stern placement also makes them totally inaccessible to the second angler in the boat. Only on larger craft with forward steering should anglers position downriggers on the stern, and then, only as a third and fourth option.

Reaching out behind the transom to try and reach the bomb and release clip in a small boat is difficult, if not dangerous. Another major problem with transom mounting is that you need to watch your rod tips for any indication of a bite and if they are right behind you it is next to impossible to see them. As a result you may miss many strikes.

I've found it's best to have your downriggers mounted on the gunwales towards the middle of the boat and pointing out at 90 degrees to the boat. In my boat, a Savage Jabiru Tracker, the downrigger on the port side is mounted so that I do not have to get up from my seat to adjust it. The bomb and clip come up right next to me at the side of the boat and I just reach down over the side to operate the clip or bring the bomb aboard. On the starboard side, the downrigger is mounted slightly forward of this so it can be operated easily by the front passenger in a similar way.

The rod holders have also been mounted to take advantage of the position of the downriggers. They are within easy reach while I'm sitting and allow me to watch the rod tips while facing forward in the direction I am steering. It takes quite a bit of thought

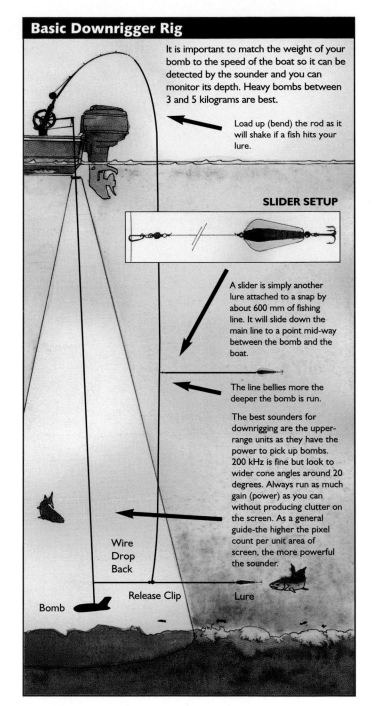

Basic Downrigger Rig

It is important to match the weight of your bomb to the speed of the boat so it can be detected by the sounder and you can monitor its depth. Heavy bombs between 3 and 5 kilograms are best.

Load up (bend) the rod as it will shake if a fish hits your lure.

SLIDER SETUP

A slider is simply another lure attached to a snap by about 600 mm of fishing line. It will slide down the main line to a point mid-way between the bomb and the boat.

The line bellies more the deeper the bomb is run.

The best sounders for downrigging are the upper-range units as they have the power to pick up bombs. 200 kHz is fine but look to wider cone angles around 20 degrees. Always run as much gain (power) as you can without producing clutter on the screen. As a general guide-the higher the pixel count per unit area of screen, the more powerful the sounder.

Wire Drop Back

Bomb

Release Clip

Lure

and trial to get things exactly right, but the results are worthwhile.

Both downriggers in my boat are also mounted on Cannon swivelling bases. This means the arms can easily be moved inboard and the bombs placed on the floor of the boat while travelling or when passing through timber, making them well worth the investment.

Be careful about placing the bombs on the floor of the boat while travelling or trailering as they can cause damage to your boat and equipment. Remember that the bombs weigh 3–5 kg and can break fishing rods etc if they roll around. A pair of old, cut-down gumboots are ideal to drop the bombs

Setting the clip on a downrigger should be done with care to ensure clean releases.

into and will stop them rolling. Some manufacturers provide hooks or cups to attach the bomb to when trolling.

Another advantage of mounting the downriggers on the side of the boat rather than the stern is that you extend the spread of the bombs (and thus the lures), cover more water and also help prevent tangling when a fish takes a lure or you turn the boat sharply.

In hundreds of hours of downrigger trolling I have found no disadvantages in having the downriggers mounted forward in the boat. I can play and net fish while still trolling and the whole operation is trouble free and relatively tangle free.

Bombs

Anglers seem terrified of big, heavy bombs and as a result, try all sorts of lighter alternatives. I have gone through this myself but have now come to the conclusion that, in most cases, the heavier the bomb you use, the better. The only limitation is the strength of your arm and that of the downrigger, to bring it up and down. In practical terms this means that a bomb weighting 2.5–5 kg is right for most applications. At this point in time lead bombs are the best, but cast iron or similar materials may soon

be required for enviromental reasons.

For slow trolling, the 3 kg bomb copes well, but it there is any speed required, such as when trolling fast minnow lures or a heavy attractor, then the 5 kg bomb is best. The heavier weight is needed to get the lure down to the correct depth and prevent it streaming back behind the boat. It also ensures that there is sufficient resistance for the fishing line to snap clear of the clip when a fish strikes. It is this resistance that makes for a nice, clean, crisp release of the line from the clip and is one of the prime requisites for successful downrigger fishing.

The bomb is usually a ball or torpedo shape and both are effective for most Australian conditions. The torpedo shape is a little more prone to snagging and I would suggest that in snaggy areas you attach the torpedo shape by the nose rather than the attachment point of the top. Rigged this way it is much less liable to snagging and the drag is unaffected although the release clip needs to be mounted on the wire rather than the back of the bomb.

Overseas anglers often paint the bombs bright or even with paint that glows in the dark in an attempt to use them as attractors and bring the fish to the lures. I have tried these ideas but the results are inconclusive.

Release clips

A good release clip must be used if you're to be successful when downrigging. For trout angling you need a delicate strike mechanism that will release lines when there is only a very slight pressure from the line yet the mechanism must also be sufficiently strong to hold the clip closed against the drag of the lure or bait. Some lures require a light release and others require a stiff release to set the hooks. Big fish need a different release pressure to small fish. This combination is available with very few types of release clips.

Clothes peg style

Some clips, like the Cannon and Magnum stacker clips, are basically like a clothes peg in that the line is clamped between two jaws which are usually coated with rubber to try to prevent line damage. These clips are effective but need careful adjustment with light line. One problem is that to be consistent with the release pressure, you need to put the line into the jaws exactly the same distance each time, which is hard to achieve when on the water. However many anglers find these release clips the easiest and most convenient to use and, to be fair, the new Magnum stacker clip is specifically developed for lighter lines of 2–4 kilograms.

Ensure that you pay close attention to loading the line into these clips and train yourself to be consistent in setting it. It is helpful to work out exactly the right position of the jaws for your line class and lures and then make a Texta mark on the rubber of the jaws so that you have some reference for the next time you set the clip.

On the plus side these clothes peg type clips are quick to set and are uncomplicated.

Button style

These clips are made in Australia by Magnum and rely on a plastic button that is threaded onto your line and then inserted into a wire jaw. When a fish hits, the button is pulled out of the wire jaw. The release tension is adjusted by physically opening or closing the wire jaws. To set these clips hold the button in the hand and let the lure trail out the back. When desired drop back is reached, twist the line five times and snap into the wire jaw. The line has to be twisted so that it will not slip through the ring and this takes time and two hands. I have used this style of clip and still do at times-it is preferable to the clothes peg type release clip but it's not the full answer.

Peg styles

The best peg style is manufactured by Scotty and works on a completely different principle to other clips. The Scotty Clip has a peg with a screw adjustment which is very precise and easily adjusted to suit a wide range of release tensions. Without effort you can adjust the peg to facilitate the release exactly to suit the lure or bait.

The line is clamped by a tapered peg, which fits into a slotted tube. It is the resistance between this tube and the peg that dictates how much resistance there will be to the release. This sounds complicated and inefficient but in practice it works excellently and very consistently.

Another huge advantage is that the peg is at right angles to the line leading up to the rod. This seems to stop the tension of the line from popping the clip while trolling along, though it releases instantly to a fish. The reason why it works is that the pressure required to release the clip is much less when exerted through the lure tow point than from above, via the line at 90 degrees.

You do need some practice to set the Scotty Clip (as you do with all clips) however you soon find that it is easy and reliable and there is little likelihood of error as each setting will release at the same pressure. This reliability and consistency make the Scotty release clip one of the best freshwater clips available to Australian anglers.

One slight problem is that when the line releases it can sometimes catch on the crimp where the trace to the peg connects to the release clip. This can be avoided in two ways. The easier is to actually mount the peg of the downrigger clip directly on your line by running your line through the hole in its head where the trace went. This is 100% foolproof but as the peg stays on the line when the clip trips, you can lose the peg if you get snagged. A soft piece of dacron trimmed tight to the knot will make it difficult to tangle on release.

Extending the release clip

It is always best to have the clip on a short wire or Jinkai leader of 26 cm as it makes an excellent bite indicator. By putting tension on the line between the clip and the rod tip, the release clip is pulled up towards the rod tip, which is bent over from the rod holder above. When a fish strikes or mouths the bait or lure, this is immediately evident on the rod tip, just like a bite in bait fishing. Detecting this movement will mean the difference between catching fish or not. The vigilant angler will note the tiny movements generated by an interested fish and will take action to arouse it into striking properly-some options would be to jiggle the rod a bit, change direction or speed, or a number of other techniques which change the lure's action. This close watch and immediate action is the secret to good catches, especially at speeds under 1.6 km/hr when trolling mudeyes.

These tiny movements also help to detect bites on sliders when a fish may take the lure and just shake the rod without pulling it out of the clip below.

Sliders

A slider is a trace with a lure attached. It is clipped onto the main line via a snap (see diagram) and slides down into the water. Water pressure generated by the speed of the boat holds the trace and lure at the middle point of your line, giving you an additional lure placed midway between the release clip below and the surface. When a fish strikes, the release clip below is triggered (or at the very least the rod is given a good shake), and the fish and both lures are brought up. I have found that Tassie lures, large wet flies and streamers provide the best results on these slider traces.

Stacking and stacker clips

Two rods or more can be used on the one downrigger but you will need to use two stacker

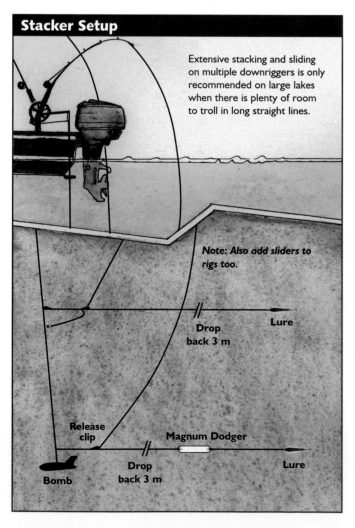

Stacker Setup

Extensive stacking and sliding on multiple downriggers is only recommended on large lakes when there is plenty of room to troll in long straight lines.

Note: Also add sliders to rigs too.

Drop back 3 m

Lure

Release clip

Magnum Dodger

Bomb

Drop back 3 m

Lure

clips to hold the lines of each rod away from the downrigger wire. Stacker clips such as the Cannon or Magnum models, have two clamps, one at each end. One clamps to the wire and the other holds the fishing line. This system allows one to stack lures onto the downrigger wire and run lures at fixed depths (see diagram).

Scotty do make small 's' plastic stoppers which can be left on the wire and wound up onto the reel of Scotty Downriggers because they have a spool sufficiently wide to accommodate these clips. On most other makes of downriggers they catch, and cannot be used.

I use a small, stainless steel clip, the type used by commercial anglers on their drop shark lines. I bought these smaller clips in Canada. Though I've not seen them here I'm sure they could be made fairly easily. I am able to hook these stacker clips instantly to the line by using a piece of valve rubber to make a tight grip and this ensures they stay at the required depth. The are also just as easy to remove.

Unless you are fishing clear deep water out of a large craft with forward controls and you are very experienced, I would suggest that most stacker clips are not worth the effort and cause far too many tangles.

Downrigging outfits

It can be a real juggling trick to raise or lower a downrigger bomb, set the release clip, steer the boat, and perhaps net a fish all at the same time. So you want an outfit that is easy to use. Baitcaster reels are by far the most suitable as you can control the line as the bomb descends more easily than with most threadline reels. A ratchet on the baitcaster can be handy as well. Baitrunner style threadline reels also have this control and are very suitable. If you use a threadline reel, keep the bail arm closed and back the drag off enough to allow the line to pull out as the bomb is lowered, but not enough to allow line to be released as a result of line drag alone. You also need to get the slack out of your line quickly when a fish strikes or even when pulling up the bomb. For this reason high speed reels are very effective for downrigger fishing.

When a fish strikes and pulls out the line from the clip, a loop of slack line is formed. Hopefully the strike has been sufficiently solid for the fish to remain hooked when the line is tightened. This can be assisted by having a fairly long, progressively tapered rod, which is tensioned right down to the water against the weight of the bomb. Not only does this allow the bites to be seen, as described in the section on release clips, but also when the fish strikes the long rod will whip up and take out much of the slack. This is why the pictures of American boats trolling shows them using rods up to 3 m which are bent right over to the water.

The release clip is fairly rough on the line, so it doesn't pay to use too light a line when downrigger fishing. Line of 3 kg breaking strain is about on the mark when trolling for trout.

Drop back

Perhaps the most common question anglers ask regarding downrigging is how much line to let out before setting the line in the clip. This depends on a number of factors-what style of lure you are using, the time of day and quality of the light, and how shy the fish are and how deep you are setting the lure or bait. As a guide, I like about 10–30 m of drop back from the bomb to the lures when fishing depths of 2–5 metres. From 5–10 m troll depth it should be shortened to 8–15 m, and from 10–20 m about 3–8 metres.

When the trout are shy you need the lures further back, yet there are times when the fish will take the lures very close to the bombs. I am sure that they are not really worried by the bomb, the motor or the boat as long as there are no undue sudden noises. Be aware too that fish (both native and trout) will come to investigate the bomb and you'll often see them doing this on the sounder.

Hum of the wire

As the bombs are dragged through the water at 6 m or more in depth and especially at the faster trolling speeds, the wire can vibrate and make a humming sound. Some anglers feel that it will drive fish away but while the hum may be annoying, there is no evidence that it scares the fish. The wire actually hums all the time but sometimes at a frequency more noticeable to the angler. If the noise annoys you there are several ways to minimise it. Try

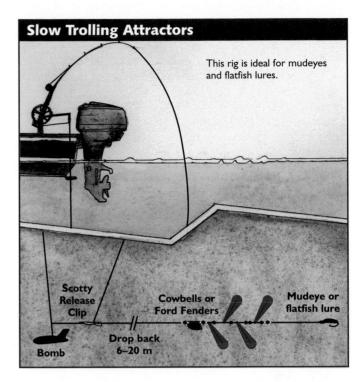

Slow Trolling Attractors

This rig is ideal for mudeyes and flatfish lures.

Scotty Release Clip

Cowbells or Ford Fenders

Mudeye or flatfish lure

Bomb

Drop back 6–20 m

mounting the downrigger on sheet rubber to isolate it from the hull, this works well on aluminium boats. You can also tie a piece of inner tube rubber from the wire to the boat to absorb the vibrations but don't forget to remove the rubber before you start to wind up the downrigger. Finally try attaching the bomb to the wire using a length of very heavy monofilament line, but monitor the wear on this line if you don't want to risk the loss of a bomb.

Positive charging of downrigger systems

I have noted that some boats catch more fish when downrigging than others and some seem never to get good results. I used to put this down to the experience of the anglers, the equipment used or just good/bad luck. Now I am not so sure.

Chinook salmon are a prime target for downrigger trollers.

Fast Trolling Attractors

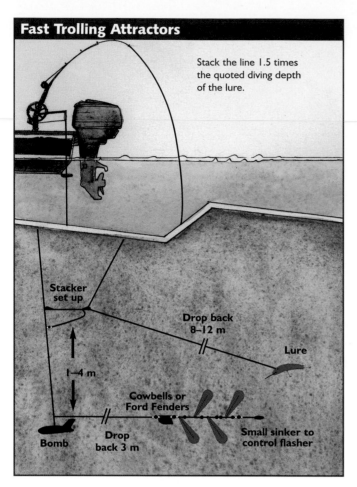

Stack the line 1.5 times the quoted diving depth of the lure.

Stacker set up

Drop back 8–12 m

Lure

1–4 m

Cowbells or Ford Fenders

Bomb

Drop back 3 m

Small sinker to control flasher

Overseas research has shown that some species of fish are extremely sensitive to weak electrical fields in the water. Trout and salmon (as well as sharks in saltwater) are species that are very sensitive to negatively charged electrical fields.

While in British Columbia I discussed this problem with the commercial skippers of the boats that used downriggers to troll for salmon and discovered that they had marine electronic circuitry installed to give their cables a slight positive charge. They even had a voltmeter connected to measure the polarity of the electrical current between the boat and the downrigger cable. Aluminium boats exhibit these voltage gaps more than fibreglass ones.

Here in Australia, much of our water is fairly mineralised and a situation can arise where the ions in the water produce an electrical current between the dissimilar metals of the boat, motor and downrigger bomb. Trout can detect these weak electrical fields. If the field produced on your boat has a positive charge around the bomb and wire then you're in luck as it has been found that trout are attracted by a positive charge of around 0.5–0.6 volts. If your boat has a negative reading and trout are repelled by a negative charge, then you might consider doing something about it.

There is an easy way to test for negative or positive charges. Simply lower the bomb about three metres into the water, connect a small voltmeter negative lead to the boat engine and the other to the downrigger wire. If the downrigger wire is positive, then 'you're cooking with gas' and the fish will not be repelled.

You can alter the electrical reading to positive by making sure the zinc anode on your motor is regularly replaced and is always in good condition. The zinc anode can also become coated with a salt when outboards are kept out of the water on a trailer. This coating will diminish the anode's function, so keep it clean for the best result.

Use a plastic snap to connect the bomb to the stainless steel wire as this helps insulate the current. Scotty and Cannon both sell their downriggers with a plastic connection clip. I always thought this was just to save money but now I realise that they had this electrical problem in mind when designing their product. Also use bombs made of pure lead, not alloys of zinc, magnesium etc which can increase the electrical current. You should use a downrigger with a plastic spool, not aluminium or similar metals, as you are trying to insulate the downrigger, wire and bomb from the metal ground of the boat.

My own boat reads just on 0.5 V and I am very happy with my catches of fish so there may be something in this theory of a positive charge attracting fish.

Electronic fish finders

The fish finder allows you to pinpoint the location and depth of the fish and the structures surrounding them; the downrigger then allows you to present your lure or bait to the exact depth of the fish. A good quality sounder will also show the position of the bomb so you can watch for snags, submerged trees, or even individual fish, and lower or raise the bomb and your lure accordingly. This ability to be in contact with and respond to what's happening under the water is the secret to downrigger success.

The best makes of fish-finders are also sensitive enough to distinguish a thermocline (a depth where there is a marked variation in the water temperature). Fish often concentrate along these thermoclines as they seek water of a more comfortable temperature and also because baitfish and plankton are found there.

On a recent trip to Lake Buffalo in the Victorian Alps, there were few fish showing in the lake, however in the depths of the old river bed my sounder revealed a thermocline line that had clouds of small fish concentrated beneath it. Patrolling

In May in Lake Jindabyne it is best to run your lures close to the bottom.

above and into this layer were fish, which were showing as distinctive arches. We trolled our lure at this depth and had reasonable success catching the redfin that were feeding on the baitfish down below.

Unfortunately not all depth sounders seem to be capable of such accuracy. For instance most of the 3D models extensively advertised will not show the bomb under the boat as these units are designed for a different application. I recommend you to go for the most powerful 2D unit that you can afford. A depth sounder that will not show a 5 kg lead weight under the boat must be missing a lot of fish as well!

To get the best readings from your depth sounder, mount your transducer on the same side of the boat as your downrigger and angle your transducer slightly backwards to put the bomb into the beam angle. Depth sounders with 18 degree transducers usually have no problems in showing the bomb but those with narrower cones may need to be adjusted. As I have my downriggers mounted forward a little in the boat, the bombs are directly beneath the transducers while in operation—an ideal set-up that helps a lot. I like to see the position of the bomb on the sounder at all times.

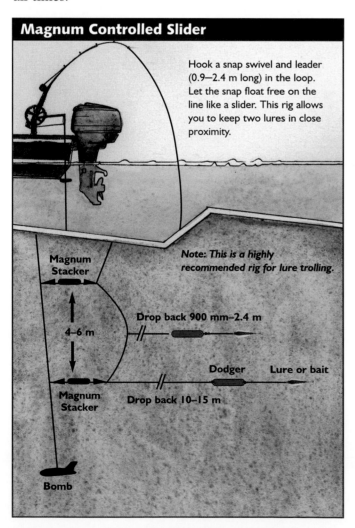

Magnum Controlled Slider

Hook a snap swivel and leader (0.9–2.4 m long) in the loop. Let the snap float free on the line like a slider. This rig allows you to keep two lures in close proximity.

Note: This is a highly recommended rig for lure trolling.

Magnum Stacker

4–6 m

Drop back 900 mm–2.4 m

Dodger   Lure or bait

Magnum Stacker   Drop back 10–15 m

Bomb

Attractors—Ford Fenders

I have found that your results can improve if you use an attractor in conjunction with your downrigger, but you must take care not to get the odd major tangle.

When you're trolling at slower speeds, a Ford Fender can be clipped onto the line in the normal way and run off the release clip provided you're using lures that work well at slow speeds, such as Flatfish, or you're trolling baits such as mudeyes or worms. Run the Ford Fender and bait or Flatfish about 6 m from the bomb. This method works well at low speed, but when the speed is increased for faster running lures, the line will not hold in the clip.

If I want to use a Ford Fender or Cowbell attractor with lures that require a faster speed, I clip the fenders directly to the bomb on a drop back of strong monofilament. This means I have to stack the lure far enough above the bomb to reduce the tangles, especially when raising or lowering the lure (see diagram).

My most effective downrigger fishing has been while using Ford Fenders and mudeyes trolled about 6–10 m behind the bomb. It is a deadly technique that takes perseverance to get right but it is deadly at times and has caught my bag limits of fish in many Australian waters.

Attractors—dodgers and chains

Dodgers, such as the effective Magnum dodger, used singly or in chains, have less resistance than Ford Fender/cowbell attractors so they can be pulled at most speeds. They are standard fare in downrigger systems when an attractor is needed. In fact there is a case to say that a dodger of some size, shape or colour should be used in front of every lure or bait trolled on a downrigger. Dodger chains are equally effective when used with trolled baits such as mudeyes or worms.

Lures, such as the Rapala CD3 styles, used with huge dodgers attached directly to the bomb are useful when trolling at speed. Arrange your lures so that they track closely behind the attractor, but be very careful when raising or lowering the downrigger.

Lures

Nearly any lure can be used on a downrigger, but some types work better than others. As the downrigger does the work in taking your lure to the selected depth, you can use even the lightest lures with sensitive actions, such as flutter spoons and the floating range of minnow lures. Of course one of the most effective lures for trout used off a downrigger is still the popular Tassie Devil.

When using a downrigger you do not need sinking minnow lures. Use the same style and patterns but in a floating version. Not only do these floaters have a slightly better action, being lighter and more sensitive, but if you have to stop the boat they float and stay clear of snags while you retrieve the lines and get organised.

All lures have their place in downrigging and it is more a case of spending the time to think about what they are going to do under water, and trolling at the right speed. The downriggers give you a versatility that was not there when you had to rely on the designed characteristics of the lure along to reach the desired fishing depths. As a general rule, you can run lures a little quicker from a downrigger than off a flatline as the water pressure is consistent all the way around it. But be careful of your spoons and Tassie Devils as it is easy to run them too fast and cause them to do full 360 degree loops, resulting in twisted lines and tangles. If your lines become twisted while trolling, you can bet you're trolling too fast for the lures. Flutter spoons are one of the lures that can be trolled really quickly.

The strike and fighting the fish

When a fish is hooked up while you're downrigging with a number of rods out, keep the boat moving forward. Don't stop or put the boat into neutral, especially if you're trolling into the wind as it will result in a memorable tangle! Keeping the boat moving forward will keep everything in order and clear, and in most cases you can actually fight the fish up to the side of the boat and land it without interfering with the other lines.

The vibration and flash of the fish being fought can also trigger a strike on one of the other lures at the same time. Usually we wind up the downrigger on the side that has had the strike so that this area is clear to land the fish.

If the fish is obviously a large specimen, then the other rods and the downriggers are retrieved and the angler is given the opportunity and freedom of an unencumbered boat to fight the fish.

Steering the boat

With plenty of hardware streaming out the back, sudden turns are out! But turns are absolutely necessary to impart extra action and attraction to your spread of lures. Don't execute full turns as they cause tangles unless the turn is taken in a wide arc. Rather, veer to the left then to the right, and speed up and slow down to impart extra action to entice strikes.

Most tangles occur when a lure is snagged or

when the angler at the helm is distracted and lets the boat wander.

Conclusions

Take the time to master the skills of downrigging and the rewards will come. Assess the realistic options of downrigging possibilities in the water you are fishing and you'll catch fish. It may be only a safe option to run one downrigger and one rod in some lakes yet in others it's practical to run multi-downriggers and many rods and lures-but don't make it difficult!

Sometimes the fish will all be on the top and the downriggers are not worth using, but more often the reverse is true and you have to get down to the fish to achieve success.

Occasionally the downriggers are outstandingly successful and there have been trips to places like Jindabyne, Eucumbene, Dartmouth, and Lake Hume where we would hardly have caught a fish without downriggers.

This kind of success, plus the interest gained in exploring new techniques, is the reason why downriggers now play such an important part in my trout trolling. *Fred Jobson, Bill Classon & Bill Presslor*

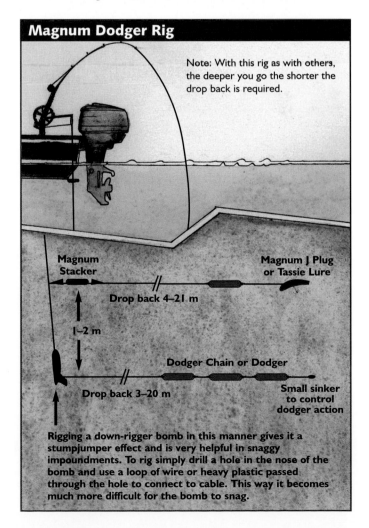

Magnum Dodger Rig

Note: With this rig as with others, the deeper you go the shorter the drop back is required.

Magnum Stacker

Magnum J Plug or Tassie Lure

Drop back 4–21 m

1–2 m

Dodger Chain or Dodger

Drop back 3–20 m

Small sinker to control dodger action

Rigging a down-rigger bomb in this manner gives it a stumpjumper effect and is very helpful in snaggy impoundments. To rig simply drill a hole in the nose of the bomb and use a loop of wire or heavy plastic passed through the hole to connect to cable. This way it becomes much more difficult for the bomb to snag.

Board Fishing

Rod holder angles best for planer board trolling are somewhere between 25° and 45°. This helps to keep the line off the water and in contact with the release clip.

The method of fishing I am about to describe consists of a contraption called a trolling or planer board. In principle, boards work much like the old mine sweepers used by the Navy. Trolling boards are operated like a downrigger, except they run out horizontally (to the side of your boat) where you can see what is going on. Instead of lowering a weight into the water, a board is placed on the water (they float) and line is released to allow them to plane off to the side of the boat.

While downriggers allow the angler to fish any depth of water, trolling boards are primarily used to fish the top five metres of water and allow lures or baits to be trolled well away from your boat (30–50 m to the side). This method has the distinct advantage of allowing the angler to run a lure or bait in undisturbed water, close to a bank, or in water too shallow for your boat to navigate.

When the fish are using the top 5 m of the water and your boat comes into it you'll find that fish do just what you'd do if you were standing in the path of a slow moving car headed in your direction—you'd move to the side and get out of the way! Fish do the same thing-get out of the path of this oncoming monster (your boat).

Any angler who has fished for any species of fish by trolling knows that your line is going to trail in the path of the boat. Your lure is going through an area of water you chased all the fish away from! For many years saltwater anglers have understood and taken advantage of this phenomenon by using outriggers to spread their lure of bait presentations.

Types of Trolling Boards

For this article we'll talk about two basic types of trolling boards:
1. Small single runner boards (in line) and
2. Double runner boards, which use a release clip like a downrigger and require a separate tow line.

The first type of boards are small planers which attach directly to your fishing line. You don't need a tow line to fish them. One of the most popular models is the Yellow Bird. These small side planers, like most boards, are sold in pairs: one runs to port (left) and the other to starboard (right). Yellow Birds attach to your fishing line ahead of the lure, and the lure is out away from the boat as far back as you wish. When a fish strikes, a release clip disengages and the small planer board flips loose, stops planing and slips down toward the lure.

On the positive side, small planers are very compact. Since you don't have to use a mast or stand pole, tow line and releases, they are easy to use. On the negative side, since they are small and light they can be unstable in a small to medium chop. Also, because of mechanical limitations, you can only effectively send a small board out 10–15 m to the side of the boat and the amount of weight you can hang on these small boards is quite limited. Another problem is that fish sometimes pull these boards off to one side when they strike, and since there is little resistance, you can miss getting hooked up. A further disadvantage of single runner boards is that when the tow line goes slack they flop over on their side which can cause tangles and false releases.

Perhaps the biggest objection to an in-line planer is that because your fishing line is never free from the board, there is considerable weight and drag on the line when playing a fish.

Nor can you effectively use light line. For many anglers both of these facets can be very discouraging. To me, double-runner trolling boards are the only way to go, and I now use them exclusively.

Double-runner boards come in a myriad of sizes and they have the ability to ride very rough water

without spinouts etc, they also do not flop over when there is slack in the tow line. Their design is such that they ride quite perpendicular to the board: even with a lot of line out they don't fall way behind the boat. When turning, they tend to keep travelling when single boards 'stall' and flop over on the inside of the turn. Also, because these boards tend to pull out at almost right angles to the boat, you can (if you have a tall enough mast or stand pole) run 30 m and more off to the sides without a lot of hassle. The biggest disadvantage with double-runner boards is their bulk, making them awkward to store. But I feel this is a small price to pay considering how well they work. While this type of board is relatively unknown in Australia at present, one manufacturer, Magnum Fishing Products, is now producing boards and complete systems.

Using trolling boards

Essentially there are three main elements to the planer or trolling board system:
1) A tow line and/or reel to hold it
2) A board and
3) A free sliding release clip, which holds your fishing line.

In addition, if you use a small tinnie for trolling you need a mast or pole to hold the tow line up in the air so that it doesn't drag through the water. After that, all you need is your rod, reel and line, lure or bait and a rod holder of some sort.

To start out (while the boat is moving) set a board in the water (first on one side of the boat and then on the other side).

Some boards are designed to be used on either port or starboard side exclusively and some are reversible. The mechanics of pull and the wedge-shaped nose design of the boards are such that as soon as the tow line tightens up the boards immediately bite into the water and plane off to the sides of the boat. Once the boards are out at the distance you want, secure the tow line and the boards simply ride off to the side.

Cast your lure or bait to the side or simply drop it overboard and release line until the lure is as far out behind the boat (dropback) as you want it, then snap the line into a release clip and attach the clip to the tow line. Now you're ready to send the fishing line off to the side.

Once again the mechanics of pull come into play. By releasing line off your reel the release clip, with your fishing line attached, automatically moves down the tow line and out toward the planer or trolling board. To stop the release clip from sliding all the way out to the board merely close the bail or stop the free-spool in your fishing reel and the

Side planing or board fishing allows the option of presenting lures well outside of the boat path and boat wake. This can be very successful if the trout are spooky or active and feeding in shallow water close to shore.

release clip stops where you want it. Set the rod in a rod holder. Your line is now out and working.

Tow lines are usually quite long (sometimes out 30 m) so you are able to run more than one fishing line on a single tow line. After you have rigged up and let out the first line simply repeat the procedure letting out a second or third line the same way. The only difference is you don't let the second line go as far down the tow line as the first, or the third line as far down as the second. Now you are ready to rig lines for the other side of the boat. The same procedure applies. You can easily run side lines from a small 3–4 m tinnie. (Be sure you check your local regulations to determine the number of lines per angler that you can run.)

If one line accidentally releases from the release clip (as it sometimes does if the tension is too loose) or if a fish hits and fails to hook up you can simply leave the board out and re-attach the line to a fresh clip. Just move the other lines over and down towards the board (you keep on trolling all the while) and reset the line again. In this way you can

let a fresh line out without bringing the boards in.

When you hook a fish you can usually leave the boards and lines out and fight the fish in the open water behind the boat. Gradually you will accumulate a number of empty clips down by the board but this is not a problem as most boards are unaffected by clips stacking up next to them. Obviously you do need to have quite a few clips at the ready to avoid having to drag the board in just to retrieve clips.

In order for your lines to release without tangling they must be 'positioned' in a definite order. If that order is in any way changed so that the various lines overlap, or if the line overlaps with the tow line, it's wipe out time! Few boats are rigged (rod holders, mast or pole etc) in exactly the same way. I can't give you a specific layout but I can explain the principles for positioning your rods in such a manner that when a fish is hooked it will swing to the back of the boat and will not (usually) cross over other lines.

To accomplish tangle-free fishing it is best to stagger your lines depth-wise (vertically) just as you do horizontally.

For example, if you're running three lines on one board, the safest way is to run the furthermost outline (the one nearest the board) the longest distance (dropback) behind the boat. Run your second line a little deeper, but not so far behind the boat. The third line is run deeper still and closer to the boat than the other two lines. In this way when you make turns, or when a fish strikes, the lines swing in such a way as to remain spread apart and so do not cross over or come into contact with each other.

Remember, if the deeper running lures and lines were on the outside you would not be able to bring them back to the boat without fouling the line so you must ensure you set up carefully. Study the accompanying illustrations carefully, they could save you a bit of grief.

Tackle and lure selection for board fishing

Rod and reel selection for use with a trolling board comes down to personal preference for your style of fishing, but I can offer a few observations and hints.

If you are going to run an attractor (dodger etc) as well as lure and bait, my preference is for an overhead reel with 3–4 kg main line. I prefer a rod from 170–215 cm and the Challenge Loomis, Penn First Strike Series and Silstar Traverse X Series all fit the bill admirably. If you choose to run a single lure or bait then a threadline reel will allow even novices to cast their line before attaching it to the release clip. This can save considerable time when rigging and allows your lures to spend more time in the strike zone. Again the above-mentioned manufacturers of rods all produce excellent models for this purpose.

In Australia we are fortunate to have a wealth of lure styles and running depths to choose from. Both shallow runners and deep divers work very effectively when used on a planer board. Shallow runners that I've had good success with include Wigstons, Thunderbolts, Tillins, Tilsan, and Magnum/Lyman lures. In deep runners, the McGraths, Tilsans, Merlins and Legends have all been productive.

One real bonus with planer boards (the double runner) is the ability to go 'down and out'. This can be accomplished by using leadline on the planer board. If you decide to try this method, tie in a short length of mono after your leadline. Put the mono into the release clip as leadline does not release effectively from any clip.

Since speed is critical in any trolling application, the lures you run and how you mix or match them can have a real impact on how successful you'll be. There are lures, plugs or spoons designed for fast, medium or slow movement. There are even times

when live bait like minnows, mudeyes or scrub worms will out-fish any other offering. Experience and continual experimentation will help enormously with your success rate.

Some useful considerations

Here are a few points to note:

1. When using boards and release clips your tow point (mast or stand pole) needs to be a minimum of 1.5 m above the water to avoid the towline dragging through the water.
2. Always make sure the line furthest from the boat has the greatest dropback.
3. Keep deep diving lures on your inside (closest to the boat) line.
4. Always have a quantity of release clips at the ready.
5. Don't be put off by choppy conditions. Any wave action is imparted to your trailing lure; the rougher it gets, the more action reaches your lure.
6. Trolling along shorelines early morning and evening allows you to target big cruising fish with little water disturbance.
7. Once you've used boards for trolling you'll soon realise that a number of factors come into play. Side planers should be used whenever water temperatures are at a level conducive to allow trout or salmon to stay in, or at least temporarily go into, this temperature level. Each species of trout or salmon has a slightly different preferred temperature range. Knowing a fish's preferred temperature range will help in targeting whichever species you're fishing for. A good temperature probe is an invaluable tool for board fishing.

Planer or trolling boards are not limited to fishing for trout or salmon. There are obvious applications for practically all fish when they are up shallow and spooky! *Bill Presslor*

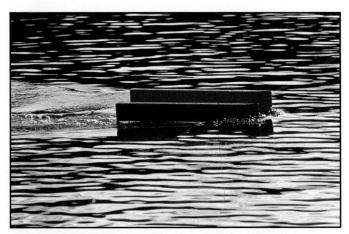

The planer board is designed to plane out and away from the boat.

Snap  Weights
For Trolling

Picture this. Your favourite bit of trolling water, rods set to a good spread with lures working a treat. Then you notice that annoying problem with your sounder. No, it's not playing up. The fish really are suspended at 8 m or deeper, hugging the structure. The lures you are running are down at 1.2 m and 3 m and, not surprisingly, you're not getting any action. But you've left the downriggers at home, and your leadcore line is nestled in the back of the ute. How are you going to get to the strike zone?

There is an alternative! Snap weight trolling was developed in North America for targeting suspended or structure-hugging walleyes, where success requires a special presentation of the lure or bait.

Downriggers are undoubtedly the best tool for precise presentations at depth, but can be costly if you are trolling in snag-infested water and you hang up your bomb on a submerged tree or rock. A snap weight line can easily be run in conjunction with a leadcore line, flat lines or downriggers. Snap weight lines are also perfect as planer board lines with either in-line boards or double trolling boards. This technique will prove a valuable asset for any dedicated troller, as it allows you to run more deep lines without a downrigger or leadcore.

At one time or another we've all tried trolling sinkers of every size and description, but each seems to have its drawbacks. If you run the weight close to the lure or bait you run the risk of spooking the fish. Too far away and you can't land the fish because the weight is in the way. Use enough weight to get you deep and it takes the fun out of landing the fish.

Snap weights overcome these problems because they employ a pinch pad release (like a downrigger release clip) with a trolling weight attached. The real beauty of

This impressive chinook salmon was taken on white Cobra with a 42 g snap weight attached. Snap weight set ups can be used in conjunction with downriggers quite successfully.

Snap Weight Table

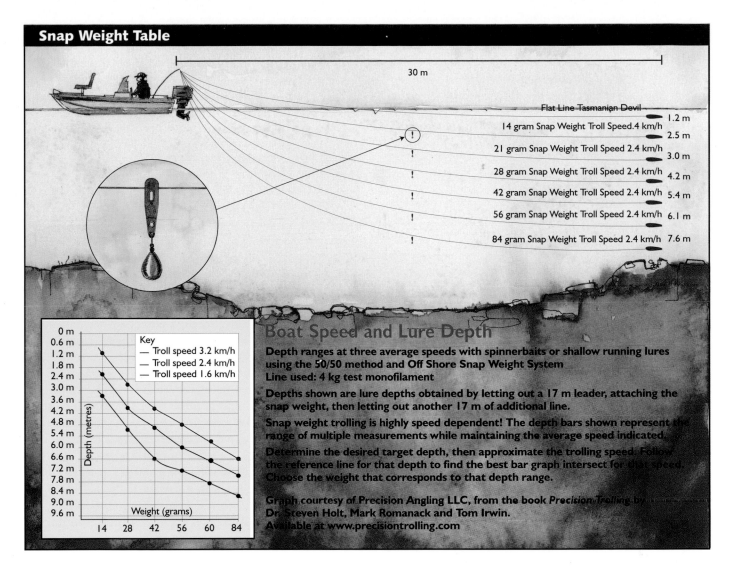

30 m

Flat Line Tasmanian Devil — 1.2 m

14 gram Snap Weight Troll Speed.4 km/h — 2.5 m

21 gram Snap Weight Troll Speed 2.4 km/h — 3.0 m

28 gram Snap Weight Troll Speed 2.4 km/h — 4.2 m

42 gram Snap Weight Troll Speed 2.4 km/h — 5.4 m

56 gram Snap Weight Troll Speed 2.4 km/h — 6.1 m

84 gram Snap Weight Troll Speed 2.4 km/h — 7.6 m

Key
— Troll speed 3.2 km/h
— Troll speed 2.4 km/h
— Troll speed 1.6 km/h

Depth (metres): 0 m, 0.6 m, 1.2 m, 1.8 m, 2.4 m, 3.0 m, 3.6 m, 4.2 m, 4.8 m, 5.4 m, 6.0 m, 6.6 m, 7.2 m, 7.8 m, 8.4 m, 9.0 m, 9.6 m

Weight (grams): 14, 28, 42, 56, 60, 84

Boat Speed and Lure Depth

Depth ranges at three average speeds with spinnerbaits or shallow running lures using the 50/50 method and Off Shore Snap Weight System
Line used: 4 kg test monofilament

Depths shown are lure depths obtained by letting out a 17 m leader, attaching the snap weight, then letting out another 17 m of additional line.

Snap weight trolling is highly speed dependent! The depth bars shown represent the range of multiple measurements while maintaining the average speed indicated.

Determine the desired target depth, then approximate the trolling speed. Follow the reference line for that depth to find the best bar graph intersect for that speed. Choose the weight that corresponds to that depth range.

Graph courtesy of Precision Angling LLC, from the book *Precision Trolling* by Dr. Steven Holt, Mark Romanack and Tom Irwin. Available at www.precisiontrolling.com

snap weights is that they allow the angler to choose how close or how far the weight is placed from the lure.

The system works by allowing the angler to determine the leader or dropback, the distance the lure or bait is let out the back of the boat. Once this is established the snap weight is simply pinched open and attached to the line. The line, with weight and lure or bait attached, is then let out further behind the boat. Simple and very effective!

Snap weights are available commercially in sizes from 0.5–3 ounces (14–84 grams). Because they consist of a release clip with a lead weight attached by a split ring, you can experiment with the whole range. I generally carry 3/8, 1/2, 5/8, 3/4, 1 and 1 1/2 ounce (7, 10.5, 14, 21, 28 and 42 gram) weights for the type of fishing I do, but I have used heavier weights as well. Remember that once you get the weight to your rod, you can unsnap it and play the fish unencumbered.

An American company called Offshore Tackle Co manufactures the best known of the commercial snap weights. If you choose to make up your own, use a cylindrical or torpedo shaped lead weight to cut down on drag. Either the Scotty Snapper release or Magnum release clips work very well for this application. Attach your choice of weight with a large split ring to the release clip, and you're ready for action.

Tackle selection

To troll with snap weights, most trout or native fish tackle will fill the bill admirably. To start out with this system, I'd suggest you look for a rod with a medium to fast action around 1.8–2.2 m in length. I use a 2.1 m G.Loomis HS9000 rod rated for 3–5 kg line. Ideally you want a rod that is tippy enough to telegraph your lure's action, but still able to cope with dragging around a bit of weight. I've had a look at the new 'Technique Specific' Walleye rods (models WJR-741-S or WJR-742-S and the WRR-8400-S) by Loomis and they would be perfect for this task. They are available on request through E.J. Todd in Australia.

Your choice of reel is really a matter of personal preference. Baitcasters, overheads, or spinning reels will all do the job, although my favourite is an overhead reel with a line counter.

Line selection for snap weight trolling is important. This technique does not require fine line diameters to help achieve depth. Keep in mind that if you're fishing an impoundment with lots of snags your line is going to get a real beating.

Look for a tough abrasion resistant line with low stretch and something in the order of 3–5 kg breaking strain. Over the years I've developed a real fondness for Platil Strong ST as a dependable trolling line. I've also used other brands such Asso and Maxima with good results.

After you have landed a fish or been snagged remember to cut a metre or two off the end of your line. Most of the stretch in mono or copolymer lines occurs near the end. Cutting a bit of line off and retying your lure or bait may save you the grief of losing a good fish. Don't leave it lying around, though—pocket it and dispose of it at home.

To make your presentation as accurate as possible you need some means of measuring the line you let off your spool. For years I counted revolutions of the spool and measured and marked my line to get as accurate a reading as possible. I now use a line counter reel that makes the task a lot simpler. Be warned, they are expensive. A less expensive method involves a clamp-on mechanical line counter that fits on your rod and measures line out after it leaves the reel. The main purpose of all these toys is to enable the angler to accurately repeat the amount of line out. If you catch a fish at a particular depth or drop-back, you can repeat the process to get back to the strike zone.

If you don't have a line counter, use a permanent marker to mark your line at regular intervals. I really can't overstress the importance of knowing how much line you have out with this technique. To avoid constant hang-ups, you need to know where your lure is in relation to the bottom or structure. Your sounder is an indispensable tool for depicting depth and structure. I use a Lowrance X-85 and I have found it an extremely accurate piece of equipment. The detail that most modern sonar units can give you is quite amazing!

Lure selection

We're very fortunate to have an enormous selection of lures to choose from in Australia. Local products such as Lofty's Cobras, Tassie Devils, Tillin's King Kobras, and minnow style lures all work well with this technique, as do Rapalas, Luhr Jensen's Quickfish and Worden's Flatfish. The snap weight system was developed to troll spinnerbaits and worm harnesses for walleye, but most minnow style lures work equally well. Just about any lure that will consistently troll on a flatline from 1–1.5 m is usually a good choice. I would steer away from using this technique with deep-diving lures, as depth prediction is just too complicated.

Don't discount bait as an alternative. A big scrubworm on a worm harness like the Luhr Jensen Wedding Ring Spinner or a Walleye Harness (yes, they do work on both trout and native species) can be deadly, especially in winter or spring when water levels are rising. Smaller bladed attractors and dodgers can be very productive when used in conjunction with bait, but with all but small dodgers it's very difficult to accurately predict depth.

Boat speed and lure depth

The most widely used application for snap weight trolling is to take a normally shallow running lure deeper. If you want to get the most out of this method, remember that snap weight trolling is highly speed dependent. The slower you go, the deeper the lure will run. This also applies to the amount of weight you use. Heavier weights are also going to take your lure deeper. A boat speed in the vicinity of 1.5 km/h is a good starting point.

The standard trolling method with snap weights is called the 50/50 system, developed by professional walleye anglers to help standardise leads or dropbacks and to more accurately predict depth. It relies on a lead of 50ft (16.7 m) being let out behind the boat, the weight snapped on and another 50ft (16.7 m) let out.

I have presented a graphical chart as a guide to get you started. With the number of variables in this system you need to consider carefully what presentation you want. The information in the graph is accurate to within about a metre.

Your own experience will soon have you working out depths accurately. Remember that your presentation will run slightly deeper than the snap weight.

Advanced applications

My personal favourite use for snap weights is running them off a planer board. By using snap weights on my planer board lines I can increase my coverage of fish because my line is not only out in undisturbed water, but down as well. This method is often very productive if your target fish are in clear water and are spooky. Natives like golden perch are prime candidates for this technique. To target fish that are suspended it is very handy to be able to run a couple of snap weight lines in addition to your down riggers.

Another application for snap weights is to place them closer to the lure and use them as bottom bouncers. Bottom-hugging fish are attracted to the lure or bait that trails behind the bouncing snap weight. This is not a technique for the faint-hearted. You can sacrifice a bit of gear to snags but you can also catch big fish. Though again developed in North America, it has enormous potential for our fishing.

Give snap weighting a go. I think you'll find you can have a great deal of success, as well as improving your catch rate! *Bill Presslor*

Trolling Attractors

Over the years I have rationalised and come to terms with the fact that while it should be enough to just be out there in the wild, it is much better when I catch a few fish.

My experience has shown me that the most deadly method of catching trout is to troll attractors. In recent years, since I've perfected the technique, I can't remember an outing when my catch was not either up with, or surpassing, those of most other anglers. I've also come to the conclusion that trolling attractors is not well understood. It requires some experience to be effective-you can't just hang those jingly-jangly things over the side and catch trout.

Attractors originated in the Great Lakes region of the United States of America in the same fishery that gave us downriggers, flutter spoons and dodgers. To my knowledge they actually preceded downriggers, having been pre-Second World War.

Although some anglers imported their own, they really came to the attention of Australian anglers when the Snowy Mountain lakes of Eucumbene and Jindabyne were newly formed. Canadian and American cowbells produced by Les Davis, Gibbs and Luhr-Jensen were used with bunches of fat scrubworms and were very effective in those fish-rich days. These 1.5 m chains of multiple spinners, aptly named cowbells, still work but are now more refined and sophisticated in design, construction and use.

Innovators such as John Novak, Victorian manufacturer of Wonder Lures, were responsible for the introduction of many lures and styles of fishing. John was well acquainted with American technology and adapted it to suit the conditions and species he found here. The original Wonder Wobbler, one of the classic Australian lures, originated in this way. On his frequent trips to the USA to research new products, John brought out the components from Luhr-Jensen and started to produce Ford Fenders and cowbells

Attractors include Ford Fenders, cowbells and dodgers and are a perfect combination to troll with spoons for trout.

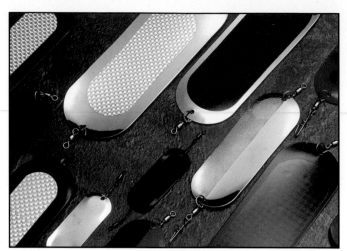

Colour can often make a big difference—try different colours to find just which one is giving the best results on the day.

here in Australia. All the components are now made in Australia.

Twenty-five years ago, I watched John Novak and Geoff Brook use wire line, baitcasters and Ford Fenders to catch bags of trout at Eucumbene when no-one else was catching anything. These experiences helped crystallise my own present day fishing styles and preferences of fishing.

General Spoon Shapes

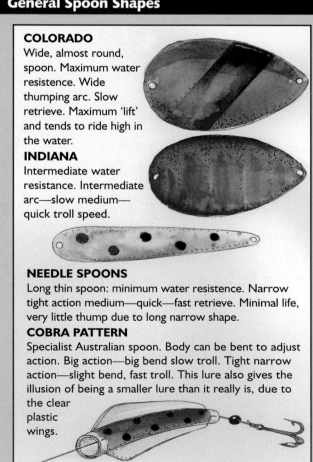

COLORADO
Wide, almost round, spoon. Maximum water resistence. Wide thumping arc. Slow retrieve. Maximum 'lift' and tends to ride high in the water.

INDIANA
Intermediate water resistance. Intermediate arc—slow medium—quick troll speed.

NEEDLE SPOONS
Long thin spoon: minimum water resistence. Narrow tight action medium—quick—fast retrieve. Minimal life, very little thump due to long narrow shape.

COBRA PATTERN
Specialist Australian spoon. Body can be bent to adjust action. Big action—big bend slow troll. Tight narrow action—slight bend, fast troll. This lure also gives the illusion of being a smaller lure than it really is, due to the clear plastic wings.

What are attractors?

Attractors are designed to bring the fish up to the bait or lure that is usually rigged in combination with the attractor. A similar set-up in salt water involves what are termed 'teaser' lures. Freshwater attractors are usually multiple spinning blades of various designs and sizes rigged in tandem on wire or cable shafts although dodgers and flashers and some big plugs can also be included. There are no hooks on the attractors as the trailing bait or lure is designed to hook the fish.

Why trout are attracted

The fact that trout are attracted to the flash, vibration, bangs and clangs on the attractor lures goes against all conventional theories, which dictate a quiet, cautious approach to trout angling. To rationalise this, it is theorised that the multiple strobe-like flashes of the blades, and the vibration and noise, simulate a school of minnows, small fish, or even the feeding of a school of trout.

A more likely explanation may simply be that in the wide deep waters of most lakes, trout represent the top of the immediate food chain and are not really preyed upon. Consequently, they are not especially cautious and will come up to an attractor lure to satisfy feelings of curiosity, aggression, hunger, excitement, school feeding competition and interest.

Like a magnet, the attractors bring the fish in close to the bait or lure and provoke the trout into striking. At Dartmouth Dam I watched a rainbow of about 4 kg repeatedly strike the spinning blades of a Ford fender and ignore the mudeye trailing 60 cm behind. Terry Ward has a story of a huge strike at Lake Hume, which resulted in the big blade being torn off his Ford Fender. This may explain some of the strikes that don't hook up while trolling attractor lures.

Type of attractors

Dodgers

Speed is fairly critical to the successful operation of dodgers—stick to the manufacturer's recommendations. These large spoon type lures wobble from side to side or spin on an axis to send out flashes and impart action to the trailing lure/bait. Their big advantage is that they are much easier to pull as there is much less water resistance. They are better for trolling lures and flies than bait as they often work best at a faster speed than bait requires.

With dodgers a short trace of about 30 cm imparts an action into the trailing lure. Small spoons and flutter spoons, with their light weight and action, are most suitable behind dodgers. Wonder 'Big Flash' and the excellent Magnum Dodgers, which come in smaller sizes more suitable for Australia, are available along with imports from America and Canada. The innovative Magnum Dodger chains work especially well, even with mudeyes, and are perhaps the best of this style of attractors for Australian conditions and fish.

Ford Fenders

The Ford Fender is the classic attractor lure for Australia and is best to use when using bait like mudeyes. The two long blades are mounted on a wire frame and they have the weight to get down deeper in the water than other attractors. The action of the big blades, spinning like a giant Celta-type lure, imparts a darting motion in the bait or lure behind.

Luhr-Jensen and Les Dais Lures from the USA and Canada make Ford Fenders with an excellent finish. They also make some four-bladed models, which are effective, but I feel they add unnecessary drag. I have cut these four-bladed models in two, making one normal two bladed set and then a smaller set that is good for light line use. Australian made Wonder Lure Ford Fenders are an excellent product that have a good finish and a wide range of colours.

Wonder Lures' Ford Fenders come in a variety of colours including silver, gold, copper, fluoro red and fluoro green as well as combinations on special orders. I much prefer combinations and can especially recommend fluoro green and silver for bright light and downrigger use and copper/brass combination for low light and medium depths.

Multi-troll and Willow Leaves

These attractors are mounted on wire cables and feature four-pointed blades, which are all the same size on the multi-trolls, and are from small to large sized dimpled metal blades on the willow leaves. This attractor is particularly good for trolling lures as they can be trolled at higher speeds without excessive drag. With a small blade on the rear of the willow leaves, the action of the lure following is not modified by the action of the attractor.

Cowbells

These attractors are also mounted on cable and offer a variety of blades that are all basically the same size. Wonder Lures have a good basic model with four rounded blades in the same colour range as their Ford fenders. Lee Davis and Gibbs offer a huge range of models, many of which have modified edges and fluoro inserts. These attractors are excellent quality and finish and are highly suitable for both lure and bait combinations. Without the addition of extra weight cowbells do not run as deep as Ford Fenders. I would particularly recommend cowbells for use in combination with worm baits and spinning lures.

Attractors - Why they work and how!

DODGERS

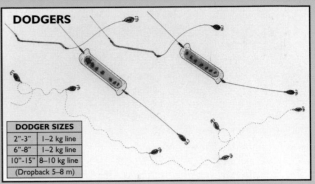

DODGER SIZES	
2"-3"	1–2 kg line
6"-8"	1–2 kg line
10"-15"	8–10 kg line
(Dropback 5–8 m)	

The dodger is simply an attractor that employs flash and sound to attract trout and salmon. It also causes the trailing lure to act very much like an injured or crippled baitfish.

FLASHERS

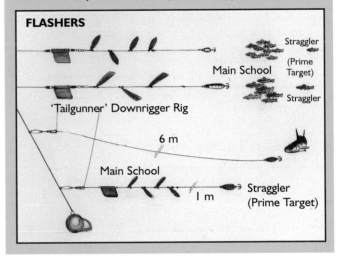

School of Minnows and Mini Cowbells

A variety of smaller blade sets of attractors are available from all manufacturers. These smaller models don't have the flash and attracting powers of the larger sets but do have the advantage of offering little resistance thus making them suitable for use with light outfits. In the creek arms and rivers, these smaller models can be effective for the very reason that they do give off less flash and vibration which scares the fish less in the smaller scale waterways. I believe one problem with these smaller bladed models is that trout may strike the blades rather than the lure/bait. This also happens with the larger models but not to the same degree.

Attractor lures are not easy to use and require a degree of skill and experience before you get to the position that they work consistently for you.

Attractor and Lure combinations

Virtually any lure can be used behind an attractor, but to be effective the lure and attractor must be capable of being trolled at the same speed.

Because of the resistance of the multiple blades it is impracticable to troll attractors at anything but the

Trolling the Lakes

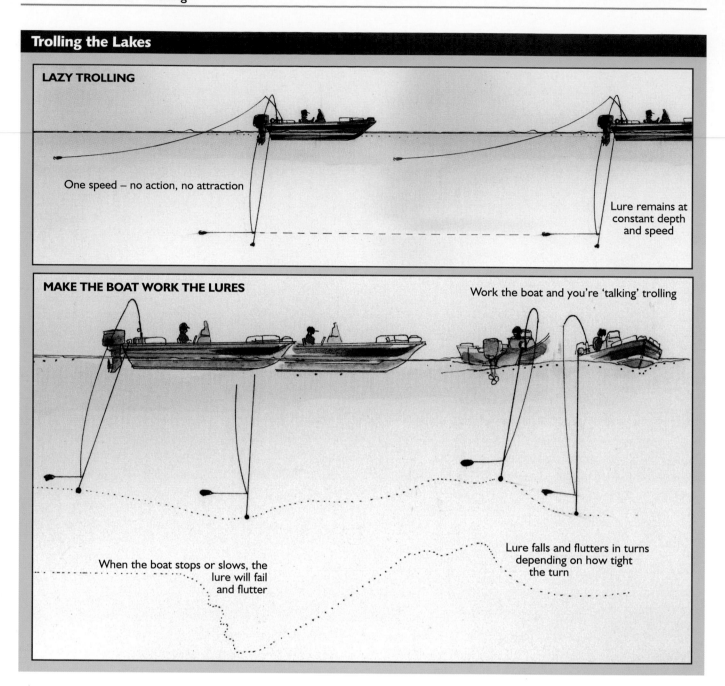

LAZY TROLLING

One speed – no action, no attraction

Lure remains at constant depth and speed

MAKE THE BOAT WORK THE LURES

Work the boat and you're 'talking' trolling

When the boat stops or slows, the lure will fail and flutter

Lure falls and flutters in turns depending on how tight the turn

slower speeds, so lures most suitable for use with the attractors should work best at those speeds. This trolling speed compatibility is even more important if you wish to run a lure on one rod and a bait on the other.

Flatfish

An F4 or F7 Flatfish on a trace 40–60 cm behind a Ford Fender or cowbell is a classic lure combination. In every trout water I have tried, this combination has caught fish. Colour selection is important here and black and gold, followed by perch scale, frog, fluoro red, and coach dog, (not necessarily in that order) have been most productive.

The Flatfish should be carefully tuned by making sure the hook and line attachment points are straight,

ensuring that the lure swims in a side-to-side wobble rather than spinning. The best speed is as slow as you can go while still getting the attractor blades to spin; faster speeds may induce spin in the Flatfish.

Spotted Dog and Minnow Lures

Surprisingly enough, some of the most effective lures behind attractors are small minnow type lures, which normally you would expect to fish at a moderate speed. The Rapala 5 cm floating minnow is the standard against which this style of lure is judged, as it is the optimum size and shape. The light floating body develops more action at slow speeds. Other suitable minnows are the Rapala CD5 and CD3, Bennett Baby Scorpions, Tilsan, Rebel Minnow and McGrath Shallow Runner.

When using these lures behind an attractor it is better to dispense with the usual clip or loop knot and tie a clinch knot directly to the lure. The clinch knot is tied to the bottom rather than the middle of the loop and is pulled up as tight as possible.

By altering the angle of line attachment the slow speed action of minnow lures is increased, making them more compatible with attractors.

Hand painted 'spotted dog' patterns seem to be the most effective for this style of fishing. They should be fished at very slow walking pace, which allows the lure to work but doesn't subject the attractor to too much water resistance.

Jointed minnow lures are also a good choice of lure because they have increased action at slow speeds.

Wigstons and Spoons

Both of these lure types work well behind attractors, usually with a slightly faster trolling speed. Manipulating the rod by hand to get an erratic action can enhance this. With some spoons you can adapt the body shape to increase the slow speed action. For example, a small Super Duper can be improved by spreading the U-shaped body. Lightweight spoons, such as Imp-types and flutter spoons are the best suited for this style of fishing. A trace of about 40–45 cm works best with these spoons.

Wigstons should have a bigger bend put in them to improve slow speed action.

Spinning Lures

Celta-type spinners work well if you sweeten the hook by adding a small worm. A silver and green size 2 Celta complete with a small worm is one of the most productive combinations at Dartmouth Dam.

In selecting a spinner, look for lightness and a freely spinning blade. The Vibrax Rooster Tails, distributed by Gillies here in Australia, are especially suitable because of their light construction and free spinning blades. Even the hooks are strong but light.

Other lures

The Rebel Ultra Light lures are all small, natural looking lures that surprisingly are suitable to use behind attractors as they have a light weight, small size and a wide, enticing action at slow speeds. The Teeny Wee Crawfish, Teeny Wee Frog, Crickhopper, Jointed Rebel Minnow and Cat'R'Crawler all work well. One problem is that the very small trebles are too small and light and should be replaced with slightly stronger and bigger trebles when used behind an attractor lure.

Attractor and Bait Combinations

Although lures work well, the most effective method is to use attractors in combination with live, fresh bait. When rigged and fished correctly this combination outfishes every other method, even on a good day. On those hard days when the fish won't co-operate it is often the only way to get a fish. During my last three trips to Jindabyne we found that a Ford Fender and mudeye combination resulted in close to bag limits each day while other methods resulted in few fish.

Mudeye Attractor Combinations

I lay claim to originating this technique in the early days of Dartmouth Dam. While it is now commonly used throughout the southern States, it is evident that many anglers do not appreciate its subtleties and miss out on the best results. It is not easy to get everything exactly right and keep it that way, so it's not a technique for lazy anglers.

The mudeye is a delicate creature and needs care to mount it correctly on the hook. A suitable hook pattern for trolling couta mudeyes is a long shank, forged, down eye, round bend hook. Mustad

This is the exact Spotted Dog adaption—you can't buy it commercially, you have to paint a Gold Rapala 5 cm floater.

model 94840 is ideal. The length of the shank and gape of the hook is dictated by the size of the mudeye. The point of the hook is inserted into the mouth of the mudeye and gradually down into the body, with the insect being forced around the bend of the hook so that the point comes out dead centre in the lower abdomen. The insect is then supported between your fingers in the right hand and the point of the hook pulled rearwards which pulls the eye of the hook and knot into the head of the mudeye.

When done properly the mudeye lies flat along the shaft of the hook and is towed, from the front, by the eye of the hook and the knot. If it curves or bunches up, the mudeye will spin, twist you line and be unattractive to the fish. Bug mudeyes can also be mounted to troll in the same way by using shorter shank hooks.

Ford Fenders are by far the best attractor lure to use with mudeyes as, at a dead slow troll pace, the throb of the large rotating blades causes the mudeye to troll through the water in short bursts, much like a free swimming mudeye. This beat or throb can be seen on the rod tip when the right speed is achieved.

The Ford Fender/mudeye combination is a technique that requires a fair amount of concentration. You cannot set and forget, which is how many anglers like to fish. You must constantly watch the rod tip as the trout can strike with a finesse that is surprising. Sometimes just the head or tip of the tail of the mudeye will be ripped off. I am sure that trout will often follow your line for quite a while, mesmerised by the flashing blades of the attractor and nipping at the mudeye. You can see little knocks and plucks at your line if you watch it closely. Other times, they will grab the mudeye and swim towards the boat, taking some of the strain off the rod tip. They can also be hooked, but rather than struggle will allow themselves to be led along like a dog on a chain. All these types of behaviour are missed if you are not vigilant.

Because of the fragile nature of the mudeye you will usually need to replace, or at least adjust, the bait if a fish has struck or you have touched a snag. If the mudeye is damaged or spinning you will not get a fish.

If you notice anything unusual on the rod tip that may be a fish, pick up the rod and try to entice the fish into striking. Altering the boat speed and giving the Ford Fender a different action often works.

Worm Attractor Combinations

Particularly during the winter months when the trout are used to feeding on worms washed into the lake, but even during the warmer months, worms are an excellent trolling bait behind attractors despite the highly artificial presentation. While Ford Fenders are the best attractors for mudeyes, cowbells and multi-trolls are equally good when using worms and offer less resistance, which lets you troll a little faster.

With normal garden worms and even the smaller scrubworms, I find it best to use two worms. The first is threaded directly through the head and then pulled up over the eye of the hook. The second is hooked a couple of times through the centre of the body, which leaves plenty of loose ends to wiggle and attract the fish. The small scrawny worms sometimes make a better bait than the bigger specimens.

These small worms are also effective when used as a sweetener on the hooks of artificial lures and can do better in combination than the worm or artificial lure by itself.

Scrubworms are too big to use when bunched up and work better when threaded up the line and kept extended by a small keeper hook. A tandem rig of hooks keeps the bait straight in the water and gives a better hook-up rate.

When used at depth behind a downrigger the attractor/worm combination is very effective and has the advantage of not being as fragile and subject to damage as an attractor/mudeye rig.

Other Baits

Very small yabbies, small wattle grubs, most large nymphs and minnows can all be used behind attractors. The main consideration is to mount them on a hook so that they stay straight and do not spin. Care with hook size and type and a little ingenuity with half hitches and small keeper hooks will enable you to swim nearly any bait in a natural manner that the trout find attractive.

Downriggers

Downrigger fishing goes hand in hand with attractor lures but presents a whole new set of problems. The drag of the attractor/lure combination requires a fair amount of resistance on the downrigger release clip to stop it constantly pulling out prematurely, but with some makes of clip this results in small and sometimes even large fish not pulling the line cleanly out of the clip. In extreme circumstances this can even result in the fish breaking the line between the bomb and the lure.

Clothes-peg releases do work if you have the experience to put the line in at exactly the right depth and the new Cannon freshwater adjustable clip is good. Even better is the Scotty Hairtrigger downrigger clip. An important modification is to mount to Scotty Hairtrigger on a short-race of up to 35 cm from the bomb. This trace, when stressed by the pull of the rod, acts as a sensor to enable you to see every little touch and strike on your lure or bait. The sensitivity

Match the Hatch

Flyfishers always look to "matching the hatch" in their selection of fly when imitating the natural insect. Do the same thing with your spoons—pick to size and shape best to the predominant baitfish the trout are after. This of course may prove difficult if you're fishing a new area. But there are some tricks to pull before actually putting the boat in the water. Obviously ask the locals and armed with that information, have a quick reconnoitre on the lakes edge. Look for any evidence of dead or floating bait in and around the shores. Look in and around weed beds for evidence of live bait, and even better haunt the cleaning area.

LURE OR SPOON SELECTION
King Cobra (No.'s) 64,65,77
Reidy's Mighty Mite
Halco Combat
Rapala Shadrap

LURE OR SPOON SELECTION
Bennett McGrath Carp
Rapala Shadrap (SR5CW)
Cordell Big O (0772 H7)
Halco Combat
Nilsmaster Invincible 8 cm (1565-3)
Yo-Zuri Hot Joker
Rapala Mini Fat Rap (MFR3GFR)

LURE OR SPOON SELECTION
Tillins
King Cobras
Wingstons Tassie Devils
Old Cobbers
Yo-Zuri Tachyon

LURE OR SPOON SELECTION
Pegron Tiger Minnow
Yo-Zuri Hot Joker
Bennett McGrath (Tiger)
Yo-Zuri Floating Diver (L-02)
Rapala Original (7P)
Rapala Countdown (CD5P)
Rapala Shadrap (SR5P)
Rebel Redfin

LURE OR SPOON SELECTION
ABU-Toby (Chrome, green, gold)
Juro Little 'T' (Chrome, green, gold)
Bennett McGrath Green Tiger
Luhr Jensen Needle Fish (083)
Teeney Terror
Nilsmaster Invincible 8 cm (1555-3)
Gibbs Candlefish
Gibbs Stewart

LURE OR SPOON SELECTION
Gibbs Needle Spoon
Killalure Pink Rainbow
Rapala Countdown (CD5 RT)
Rebel Rainbow
Bennett McGrath Rainbow
Luhr Jensen Flutter Spoon
Luhr Jensen Salmon Seeker (314)
Gibbs Candlefish

LURE OR SPOON SELECTION
Gibbs Needle Spoon
Rebel Brown Trout
Luhr Jensen Flutter Spoon
Gibbs Candlefish
Luhr Jensen Salmon Seeker (330)

is not absorbed by the bomb and downrigger, making this style of fishing much more effective.

In practice, you can actually see the bites on the rod tip in a manner very much like bait fishing and you then pick up the rod and strike it out of the clip to hook the fish.

Fishing outfits

Getting the right rod is very important. The best rods have a parabolic action—that is, their taper continues to bend further down the rod than the fast, tippy rods which have little flex in the bottom half. Baitcasters are also superior to threadline reels as they allow you to gradually drop the attractor back without tangling.

Line and traces

Four or five kg line can be used from the reel to the attractor. This relatively high breaking strain line will not put the fish off, as it is the line from the attractor to the bait/lure that the fish see. The stronger main line gives you a chance of retrieving snagged attractor lures and releases more cleanly from the clip than with ultra-thin line. I prefer my main line to have very little stretch so it transmits, with sensitivity, any strikes or nudges that would be absorbed by a line with more spring.

Quite the opposite is required from the trace. When a fish first strikes there is a lot of strain imposed on the trace because of the resistance of the attractors, so you should not use a light trace. Four kg breaking strain is ideal and you should look for a trace line that has a lot of stretch. In the Great Lakes in America they tie in short elastic shock traces to stop the initial shock of the strikes, and the stretching trace does the same thing.

Usually a trace length of 40 cm

Parabolic rods and baitcasters are best for attractor trolling.

is sufficient but if the trout are shy I have found that varying the trace length, even to 1.75 m may be needed with mudeyes. Worms and lures usually require a shorter trace.

Reel drag

A compromise between a tight and a slack drag is needed but it is an error to have to slacken a drag at the initial strike as the trout may just run with the line and then reject the bait. For the initial strike, I prefer about the same drag as you would have on the reel when spinning, and then slacken it off to play the fish gently.

Setting out the lures

It is critical how you set a pattern of lures because attractors are very prone to tangling and must be let out and trolled in the right order to prevent tangles that only a knife can solve. By setting a pattern of vertical and horizontal dispersal you can easily troll four sets of attractor lures without undue tangling, although the angler who says he never gets tangles must never put them in the water.

How the lures are set will depend on how the fish are feeding on that particular day. If the fish are deep, each angler should put one set of attractors on the downrigger with about a 7 m dropback (more or less) and then let out his other rod with a small sinker in front of the attractor keel. This sinker will alter, downwards, the angle the attractor will run through the water and take it down to about 4 m or more when run 40 m behind the boat. The rod with the weighted keel should be kept at right angles to the sides and as far out as possible. This is because when a fish strikes the attractor combination on the

downrigger it will rise to the surface; you need the other line off to the side so that it doesn't tangle.

By using both rods this way you each have two sets of attractors running at a fish-catching depth but spaced behind each other. Usually this gives you enough depth but if the fish are very deep the same spacing works with stacker clips at a greater depth.

When the trout are on or near the surface, set one rod back about 50 m behind the boat with the rod set at right angles and as far out from the boat as possible. Set the second rod only 20 m behind the boat but with the rod tip in line with the sides so that your line and the lure will track in line with the rod tip. You can also run the shorter lines on the downriggers but at only a metre or so deep, which keeps them clear of the other rod.

The different combinations of lines without weights, with weights, on downriggers, deep and shallow, in close and far out, gives you enough variation to suit the feeding pattern for the day. Experiment until you start catching fish.

Fighting the fish and boat technique

With all this hardware out, you can get into some terrible tangles if you don't take care. Every turn and variation to straight course has elements of the threat of tangling, so don't indulge in any radical boat manoeuvres.

The trout respond to changes in direction and speed but you must achieve this within the constraints of the attractor and lure's speed limitations and their set-up. Speed up, slow down, pull your lures with the rod and release them, jink the boat-but don't tangle your lures.

When a fish is hooked, the weight of the attractors makes it relatively easy for them to throw the hook, especially if they jump, so try to treat them gently and keep them in the water. I rarely wind in the other lines when we hook a fish as I find that a gentle, low-key fight results in many fewer fish lost. Just wind the fish in gently and try to steer it away from the other lines. With a bit of experience and skill you and your partner will work together to net the fish without panic and make it look easy. You may have to knock the motor out of gear a few times as you wind in the fish but bear in mind that the boat should be going forward at all times because of the other lures trailing behind.

Attractors, they rattle and bang, pull like half a house brick, and do take some of the fight and sport out of the fish-but attractor lures are the most deadly method I know to catch trout species in lakes. They have meant success for me on many trips when other methods would not have turned a scale. *Fred Jobson*

Weighted Trolling Lines

Weighted trolling lines offer significant advantages to anglers trolling lakes in the warmer weather.

When I tell people just how many fish I catch using leadline they often reply, 'I never use leadline because it takes the fight out of the fish!' Yet these same anglers head off with cowbells or Ford Fenders when they go fishing. If you have ever used these attractors you'll know what to take the fight out of a fish really means!

Landing a fish using leadline could be compared to landing a fish using a sinking 8-wt flyline, as 30 m of sinking fly line is about the same weight as 30 m of 8 kg leadline

Freshwater anglers, especially those who troll for trout, know how effective a weighted line, like leadcore line and 'unleaded leadcore' line, is for catching fish when they are holding in water deeper than the average lure will dive. Leadline is particularly useful when fishing with beginners, as these anglers are often confused if too much information, such as the mechanics of downriggers and the like, is given to then at once.

What is leadcore line?

Leadcore line is a weighted line that consists of a thin lead wire surrounded by an outer casing, usually Dacron.

The amount of lead put in the centre of a leadcore line is the same regardless of the breaking strain of the line. However the thickness of these lines increases as the breaking strain increases. This means that heavier lines experience more drag through the water and won't troll as deeply as the lighter breaking strain lines. At best a leadcore system will pull a standard 13 gram Tasmanian Devil down to around 4 or 5 metres.

Leadcore line commonly comes in 100 yard (91.4 metre) spools and each 10 yard (9.14 metre) segment is dyed a different colour. Generally speaking, the more leadcore line one lets out, the deeper the lure travels. A simple equation to follow is that for every colour of line let out, your lure will be dragged approximately one metre deeper.

What is 'unleaded leadcore' line?

'Unleaded leadcore' line is a weighted line that does not use lead to provide the weight required. Instead the line is made by braiding monofilament over 2% antimomium and 98% tin core. The line is only 66% as dense as lead so while it will almost get down to the same depths as leadcore line, it does take a little longer. 'Unleaded leadcore' was developed to combat the ban

by some countries on the use of lead in their lakes because of environmental concerns. To obtain the same depth as leadcore line quickly, you need to troll your 'unleaded leadcore' line at least one kilometre an hour slower than leadcore line. Of course this means that you may change the action of the lure being trolled.

The outer covering of 'unleaded leadcore' line is also coloured differently every 10 metres, so it is easy to tell how much line you have out. Unleaded leadcore is available in 18 lb (8.18 kg), 27 lb (12.27 kg) or 36 lb (16.36 kilograms) in spool lengths of 100 metres.

So far only J.M. Gillies have imported this type of line from Cortland.

Tackle for leadline

Spinning or threadline reels are unsuitable for leadline. The core of the leadline, being made of soft and brittle metal, tends to break with the constant twisting action of these reels, eventually breaking through the dacron covering.

Centrepin, baitcasters and revolving drum reels (or even a large fly reel), especially if they have a large diameter, are more suitable. The size of the reel will determine how much line and backing you can fit on the reel and ultimately how deep you can reach.

As for rods, don't go for a rod with a too heavy action. A 2 m medium action rod is ideal for trolling leadlines. The softer tip on most trout trolling rods often bounces backwards and forwards under the leadline load. This imparts extra action to the lure, often dropping the lure back to a following fish.

Suitable leadline trolling rods have a soft tip and load up about half way down the blank when you need to put the pressure on a fish. They must be tough enough to take the weight of the leadline but still forgiving enough to absorb the shock from a suddenly diving fish.

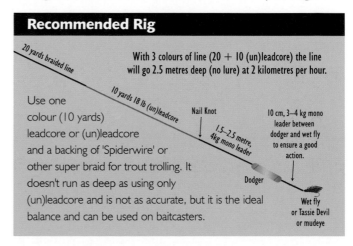

Recommended Rig

20 yards braided line

10 yards 18 lb (un)leadcore

Nail Knot

With 3 colours of line (20 + 10 (un)leadcore) the line will go 2.5 metres deep (no lure) at 2 kilometres per hour.

Use one colour (10 yards) leadcore or (un)leadcore and a backing of 'Spiderwire' or other super braid for trout trolling. It doesn't run as deep as using only (un)leadcore and is not as accurate, but it is the ideal balance and can be used on baitcasters.

1.5–2.5 metre, 4kg mono leader

Dodger

10 cm, 3–4 kg mono leader between dodger and wet fly to ensure a good action.

Wet fly or Tassie Devil or mudeye

Depths Achieved

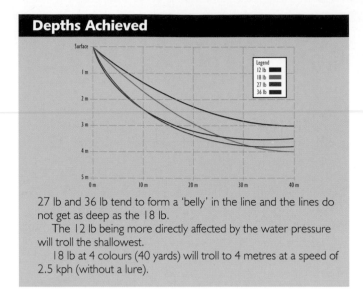

27 lb and 36 lb tend to form a 'belly' in the line and the lines do not get as deep as the 18 lb.

The 12 lb being more directly affected by the water pressure will troll the shallowest.

18 lb at 4 colours (40 yards) will troll to 4 metres at a speed of 2.5 kph (without a lure).

Rigging up

It is essential if only running 4 colours (40 m) of weighted line to add some backing. Try to match the breaking strain of the backing to that of the weighted line (e.g. 8 kg main line use 8–10 kg backing). Dacron or Micron fly line backing is ideal. However, the last year or so I have started to use some of the braided lines. They help get your line deeper because, unlike Dacron, they do not hold the water.

Backing and leader connections

While it is possible to attach the backing and leader to your main line by the use of a nail knot, I have found advantages in using a fly line 'Loop Connection Kit' available in tackle stores. Place a loop kit onto each end of your line and this will make it easy to connect when you have to change your line around.

Place a bit of Supa-Glue on the end of your line and let it dry hard before trying to place the main line into the loop connection. This will help fix the outer covering to the inner and stop it from slipping.

Once the backing and line are attached to the spool you will need to add a leader—three to five metres of monofilament (sometimes I will go up to 10 m) of a lower breaking strain than the weighted line. If you are using 8 kg weighted line then a 4–5 kg monofilament leader will be okay.

If you are using Dacron backing measure it out in 10 m segments and make each segment a different colour using a waterproof permanent marker pen. This is more important if you are only going to use three or four colours of weighted line on a baitcaster as it is a simple way of keeping track of the depth you are fishing.

Lures for leadline

All lures can be trolled on leadline. If you are using a deep diving lure then a long monofilament leader will allow the lure to dive deeper, below the leadline.

The best lures to use are those with a strong action. If a lure doesn't have a strong action then try using it in conjunction with a dodger to increase its action.

Winged lures are excellent for leadline trolling as their natural side-to-side swaying action combined with the forward/backward caused by the rod with the leadline produces a deadly action.

Baits and flies can be trolled with leadlines and there are no tricks, just keep the speed dead slow. Try using an electric motor or drifting with the wind. Remember to use dodgers or other attractors, and that the slower you go, the deeper the leadline sinks.

What is to be learned?

Trolling weighted lines is simple and hassle free. The outfit needed to operate a weighted line, is not expensive or complex and the average person on the street can afford one. By combining different lures and attractors such as Ford Fenders and cowbells, changing trolling speeds and concentrating on your sounder, leadline fishing can be very productive. *Steve Williamson*

Leadcore/(un)Leaded

Brand	Breaking Strains (kg)	Length (metres)	Colours (metres)	Contact
Cortland Kerplunk	6.36, 8.18, 12.27, 16.36, 20.45, 27.27	45.7, 91.4, 2 x 91.4 m	1 per 9.14 m	J.M. Gillies 03 9646 4745
Cortland Unleaded Leadcore	8.18, 12.27, 16.36	91.4 m	1 per 9.14 m	J.M. Gillies 03 9690 4711
Platil Lead Core	5.45, 8.18, 12.27	27.42 and 91.4 m	1 per 9.14 m	Basser Millyard 02 9695 7799
Northern Sports	6.82, 8.18, 12.27, 16.36, 20.45	91.4 and 182.8 m	1 per 9.14 m	Gus Veness 02 9540 2955
Western Filament	8.18, 12.27	91.4 m	1 per 9.14 m	Juro 03 9555 5433